HISTORICAL
FUNDAMENTALS
AND
THE STUDY OF
RELIGIONS

Historical Fundamentals and the Study of Religions

HASKELL LECTURES DELIVERED AT THE UNIVERSITY OF CHICAGO

KURT RUDOLPH

with an introduction by
JOSEPH M. KITAGAWA

MACMILLAN PUBLISHING COMPANY
A Division of Macmillan, Inc.
NEW YORK

Collier Macmillian Publishers
LONDON

Macmillan Publishing Company
866 Third Avenue, New York, NY 10022

Collier Macmillan Canada, Inc.

Library of Congress Catalog Card No.: 85-8974

Printed in the United States of America

printing number
1   2   3   4   5   6   7   8   9   10

Library of Congress Cataloging in Publication Data
Main entry under title:

Historical fundamentals and the study of religions.

   Bibliography: p.
   Includes index.
   1. Religions—History—Addresses, essays, lectures.
I. Rudolph, Kurt.   II. Title: Haskell lectures.
BL87.H56 1985   291   85-8974
ISBN 0-02-927190-8

Contents

Introduction

In 1894, Mrs. Caroline Haskell, "in hearty agreement with the conviction that the immense interest awakened by the wonderful [World's] Parliament of Religions [held in Chicago in 1893], makes it eminently desireable that students in the University, and the people generally, shall be given wise instruction on this most important of all subjects,"[1] offered a fund to the new University of Chicago to establish the Haskell Lectureship in Comparative Religion. Since that time, the study of religions in America has followed a course that neither Mrs. Haskell nor her spiritual inspirator, Dr. John Henry Barrows (organizer of the Parliament), could have foreseen. The self-confidence in the manifest destiny of Western Christendom to dominate the world's religious scene that underlay the comparative religious endeavor at the turn of the century has vanished. Comparative religions gave way first to a critical, historical study of religions narrowly conceived, then to a humanistic "science" of religions with broader as well as critical interests. Since the end of World War II, intense interest in Asian cultures, including Asian religions, has led to an amazing if nonuniform proliferation of departments of the history of religions and religious studies in American colleges and universities.

The lectures established by Mrs. Haskell have contributed to this growth and development in at least three ways. First, they have provided strong impetus to the development of an "American religious scholarship." In contrast to the situation at the turn of the century, American scholars of religion are no longer forced to travel to Britain or to Germany to receive advanced training. Second, the Haskell Lectures have helped emancipate the study of religions from the training of ministers, priests, and rabbis in "denominational" seminaries. Today, religion can be, and is, pursued as a serious academic subject in American colleges and universities. Finally, these lectures have helped overcome any isolationism threatening American religious scholarship by bringing non-American scholars of the highest caliber to the United States, scholars such as J. J. M. de Groot, Franz Cumont, Masaharu Anesaki, Sarvapelli Radhakrishnan, Hamilton A. R. Gibb, Louis Massignon, Friedrich Heiler, and Mircea Eliade, who, as an added bonus, decided to remain and teach in America.

The Haskell Lectures that Professor Kurt Rudolph, then of Karl-Marx University, Leipzig, delivered at The University of Chicago in 1983–1984, continued especially this third tradition. A recognized expert on Gnosticism and especially the baptismal sect of the Mandaeans in Iraq and Iran, Rudolph represents a venerable German tradition of the history of religions (*Religionswissenschaft*). Under the influence of liberal Protestantism and a hermeneutics of cultural retrieval, there developed in Germany a well-known tradition of the study of religions whose concerns mingled the theological and philosophical with the historical. Beginning with Friedrich Schleiermacher, that tradition culminated in the work of the famous Marburg philosopher of religion Rudolf Otto, whose book, *Das Heilige* (*The Idea of the Holy*), has had such a tremendous impact in Germany and abroad. At the same time, however, Germany has nourished a long-standing tradition of critical, philological and historical scholarship that was eventually applied, with good result, to the study of religion. Theoreticians of this tradition have consistently sought to separate the history of religions (*Religionswissenschaft*) from the philosophy of religion (*Religionsphilosophie*) and theology. Such a distinction was advocated in masterful fashion in 1924 by the young Joachim Wach who, however, unlike historians strictly speaking, sought to replace theological and philosophical reflection with an empirically grounded systematic study of religion (*systematische Religionswissenschaft*).

Professor Rudolph's theoretical remarks stand squarely within the historical, philological tradition that German scholars have practiced with such rigor and energy. As is true of any speaker addressing an audience that belongs to a life-world other than his own, Rudolph's views may not immediately meet with total assent from American students of religions whose sympathies have recently been nurtured, by and large, on the questions and categories of cultural anthropology. But as a well-studied, well-reflected, and cogent presentation of a significant position in the history of religions, Rudolph's lectures deserve careful consideration. In the first lecture, he provides a synopsis of a microcosmic manifestation of the German tradition of *Religionswissenschaft*—*Religionswissenschaft* at Leipzig—that he has discussed in greater detail for the German audience.[2] Acknowledging the formative influence of this tradition on his own thought, Rudolph proceeds in his second lecture to spell out in some detail his conception of the history of religions. The third and fourth lectures discuss the present state, internal and external, of the history of religions so conceived. The third lecture attempts to address crises of autonomy and integrity that threaten to fragment the discipline and disperse its remnants among the human studies. The fourth draws out some possible (indirect) socio-(political) implications of an autonomous and integral history of religions and, in doing so, takes up a topic that has recently attracted the attention of American scholars of hermeneutical or critical bent, the critique of ideologies *(Ideologiekritik)*. The final lecture discusses the single most important problem for a historically grounded history of religions *(Religionswissenschaft)* that wishes to avoid limiting itself to isolated details: the problem of change, or rather, of significant, interconnected changes, the problem of development. Together, the five lectures present in broad vision a significant option—if one not always seriously discussed theoretically among American students—for the history of religions as a discipline.

For his vigorous plea for historical fundamentals in the history of religions, we who heard Kurt Rudolph speak at The University of Chicago are grateful.

JOSEPH M. KITAGAWA
for the Haskell Lecture Committee

Preface

It is my pleasant duty to thank The University of Chicago, especially The Divinity School, for its invitation to deliver the Caroline Haskell Lectures. I had already received the invitation, along with an offer to serve as visiting professor in The Divinity School for half a year, in 1981. It was three years before I received permission to accept the invitation from the university with which I was then affiliated. My stay in Chicago, from September 1983 to June 1984, was one of the high points of my academic life. Not only did I come to know there for the first time the impressive academic community that exists between teachers and students at American universities; I also became aware that here my discipline—the history of religions (*Religionswissenschaft*)—was not the insignificant marginal discipline to which it had shrunk at Leipzig but formed an important part of academic instruction. This experience, and others of which I cannot take account here, were of decisive, existential significance for my future life: I now work at an American university, to continue the Leipzig tradition of the history of religions in the spirit of my teachers.

Having the option of selecting as the topic for my Haskell Lectures either a theme from my specialty, the world of late antiquity, or a methodological problem in the discipline as a whole, I chose the latter, in view of the often still uncertain shape of the history of religions in America. I have reached back to several older works of mine, published, in part, in lesser known journals such as *Kairos*.[1] The Haskell Lectures gave me the welcome opportunity not only to revive and revise these works but also to gather them together in their concern for a common theme and to place them before the English-speaking world. There is a certain sense of tragedy in doing so, for the lectures constitute a sort of swan song to my time at Leipzig which, counting my days as a student, lasted thirty-five years. At the same time, however, they mark the beginning of a new academic life that is filled with hope.

For this and for the many enriching experiences that my time in Chicago brought, I would like to offer my heartfelt thanks to the faculty and students of The Divinity School, above all to Dean Franklin I. Gamwell, Professor Joseph M. Kitagawa, and Professor Hans Dieter Betz. That the German original underlying the English is not more immediately apparent I owe to the untiring readiness and help of Gregory D. Alles, graduate student at Chicago and now instructor at Valparaiso University. I thank the faculty secretaries at The Divinity School for assistance that was always gladly given. Thanks are due, too, to Cindy Wilson of the Department of Religious Studies, Santa Barbara, for preparing the final manuscript of the lectures for the printers, and to Mr. Alles, who did the same for the notes and read the proofs. Finally, I would like to thank the publisher, and especially Mr.

Charles E. Smith, for including these lectures among its
publishing ventures.

KURT RUDOLPH

January 14, 1985
University of California, Santa Barbara

HISTORICAL
FUNDAMENTALS
AND
THE STUDY OF
RELIGIONS

LECTURE
ONE

The Leipzig Tradition
of
Religionswissenschaft

A famous dictum of Wilhelm Dilthey states, "What man may be, only history tells him."[1] Religions are important facts of history. They are part of our historical research and reflection. Inasmuch as they have affected and will continue to affect people and communities in very distinct ways—as attempts to find and explain the meaning of human existence; as factors that integrate human society and motivate human beings to think about the transcendent—religions deserve special attention. The investigation of religions by historical means is the task of a rather young discipline known as *Religionswissenschaft* or, in the rough English equivalent that I will use throughout my lectures, "the history of religions." This discipline's difficult beginnings and the history of its thorny relations with the other humanities, above all with theology, continue to burden it. According to

Joseph M. Kitagawa, the discipline has not yet assumed a very definite profile in the United States, although there have been people with very clear notions of what it was about. In a recent address in Colorado, Kitagawa spoke of a "muddled relationship between religious and theological studies as one of the unresolved issues before those concerned with the task of revisioning the study of religions in our time." He suggested that the history of religions "might play a more central role in religious studies in the future." John F. Wilson has discussed this potential role in a striking manner: "A common feature of most reflection about future study of religion is the candid presumption that history of religions may provide an overall coherence and orientation possibly absent at present in the field of religious study."[2]

I have taken as the theme of my Haskell Lectures not a special problem in the comparison of religions nor a topic from my area of specialization—the religions of late antiquity and the east-Aramaic world—but the conception of the history of religions that has guided my work in the field over the last twenty-five years. In doing so, I return to work I have already done and gather it together here for the first time. My aim is to emphasize the eminently historical character of the history of religions (*Religionswissenschaft*), a historical character inherited from the revolution in historical consciousness that occurred in the eighteenth and nineteenth centuries.

To be a historian means to think and to work methodically. To that enterprise belongs the often overlooked task of understanding one's own standpoint as a historical being. Reflection on one's own point of view belongs to historical work as much as does research. Not only may such reflection make the perspective of each historical writing clear; it leads to a broadening of one's own perspective as one enters into discussion with the perspectives of others. The dialectical action of self-reflection, criticism, and the experience of the historical object is of great importance for religio-historical work.

Therefore, I begin these lectures by portraying the tradition of the history of religions at Leipzig as I came to know it in the university's archives and through personal experience. That tradition is part of my own historically conditioned consciousness, still shaping my conception of the discipline I practice. By describing the Leipzig tradition, I also provide a glimpse of a tradition of scholarly work at one of the oldest German universities. The university at Leipzig was founded in 1409 by professors and students who left Prague following trouble with the Bohemian academic community. Since 1951, the university has been known as the Karl-Marx-Universität.

The history of *Religionswissenschaft* at Leipzig divides into two periods: the time before and the time after 1912, the year that the department and the professorial chair in the history of religions were founded.[3]

Before 1912, the history of religions was almost exclusively the concern of the humanities faculty (the *philosophische Facultät*). At the end of the eighteenth and the beginning of the nineteenth centuries, various courses on mythology, both philological and philosophical, dominated the field. Several scholars worked along these lines: Christian August Crusius, Christian August Clodius, and Friedrich August Carus in the late eighteenth century, and in the next generation Christian Hermann Weisse (1801–1866), at that time Leipzig's most important philosopher, and Gottfried Hermann (1772–1848), Friedrich Creuzer's opponent and Max Müller's teacher.

But it was the first Egyptologist at Leipzig, Gustav Seyffarth (1796–1885), who taught the University's first course in *allgemeine Religionsgeschichte* (general history of religions) in the winter term of 1841–1842. He repeated the course regularly over the years. As early as the summer term of 1832

Seyffarth had announced a course on "The History of Ancient Religions, especially Egyptian, Greek, Roman, Phoenician, Persian, Indian, and Other Religions." Seyffarth was, however, no model historian of religions. His work was completely uncritical and dominated by theological and biblical interpretations. His fate as an Egyptologist was not much better. He fanatically opposed Champollion's decipherment of Egyptian hieroglyphics, an opposition that continued unabated until his death in New York in 1885.[4]

With Seyffarth, then, the history of religions at Leipzig began rather inauspiciously. But with its next practitioner, the young discipline took a definite step forward. Karl Rudolf Seydel (1835–1892), a philosopher, offered the first of several courses on "The General History of Religions" in the winter semester of 1865–1866. His book, *Die Religion und die Religionen*, published in Leipzig in 1872, gives some idea of what he taught. As a philosopher, Seydel sought to summarize in comprehensive fashion the results of various specialized studies. Underlying his systematic treatment were his theological convictions that Christianity was the end toward which all religious development tended and that the highest religious ideal was the "perfect God-man" (pp. 142, 163–64). As he put it: "The religion of Jesus is that last, highest Unity into which all the separate streams of pre-Christian history finally flow" (p. 140). Nevertheless, Seydel's work did not lack merit. He had a good knowledge of individual religions, and he took into account the latest specialized research available to him. He advocated a frank, critical, historical study of the Bible. In fact he applied his knowledge of the history of religions to the study of the New Testament. Beginning in 1882, he published several writings that tried to demonstrate the influence of the legend of the Buddha on the original gospel.[5] This theme, which Seydel was the first to touch upon, has occupied scholarly attention from time to time up to the present.

Bruno Lindner (1853–1930), a specialist in Iranian studies, continued Seydel's tradition in the history of religions. A first-class philologist, Lindner was lecturer in Aryan Languages and religions at Leipzig from 1887 until his retirement in 1919. He regularly offered a course entitled "The General History of Religions" or "Introduction to the General History of Religions." His courses attracted a relatively large number of students, but because of an eye disease that eventually resulted in complete blindness, he did not publish much. He contributed an article, "Grundzüge der allgemeinen Religionswissenschaft auf geschichtlicher Grundlage," (Foundations of the general history of religions along historical lines) to the third edition of Otto Zöckler's *Handbuch der theologischen Wissenschaften* (Munich, 1890) that is still worth reading. His account is not free from theological convictions; for him, the "consciousness of God" was the foundation of religion, and Christianity its perfect form. Nevertheless, he remarked that the history of religion could not determine "whether the claims of a particular divine revelation are justified or not" (p. 578), and he showed critical foresight and a prudent caution toward uncertain theories. Moreover, Lindner explicitly stressed the independence of the history of religions, and he demanded that each historian of religions engage in research on a particular culture, "since," he said, "the history of a religion can be understood only if it is considered in connection with the development of an entire culture" (p. 570). Lindner thought it purposeless to engage in speculation about the origin of religion. "There is no historical research that reaches back to the beginning of historical development. . . . All history," he remarked, "deals not with individuals but with humanity divided into peoples [*Völker*]. A time before the separation of humanity into specific peoples or tribes lies beyond the ken of history" (p. 572).

Seydel and Lindner were the two chief representatives of the history of religions at Leipzig during the nineteenth cen-

tury, but they were not the only scholars who engaged in
religio-historical work. Activity in several special fields of
investigation was extraordinarily productive. Especially in
the rapidly rising discipline of Oriental studies, important
scholars treated themes of the history of religions in both
their research and their teaching. Among them were the great
Arabic scholar Heinrich Leberecht Fleischer, the Indologist
Hermann Brockhaus, and Friedrich Delitzsch, the pioneer of
Assyriology who several times discussed "the OT in the light
of cuneiform inscriptions." Others included Heinrich Zimmern, Delitzsch's pupil and successor, the Islamicist August
Fischer, Ernst Windisch, who lectured on Indology, especially Buddhology, and the champion of East Asian
philology, August Conrady. Among archeologists and clas-
sicists, Otto Jahn and Johann Adolf Overbeck for a long time
made Leipzig the center of the so-called art-mythology
school (Kunstmythologie), but it was not until Theodor
Schreiber and Erich Bethe that, strictly speaking, religio-historical work in classics began. Nordic scholars such as
Theodor Möbius and particularly Eugen Mogk devoted their
attention to the study of mythology and the history of
religions. Finally, I must mention Wilhelm Wundt
(1832–1920), who began his work at Leipzig in 1875. Wundt
taught on Völkerpsychologie for the first time in the winter
semester of 1883–1884, and two years later he offered for the
first time a course, which he often repeated, on "The Psychology of Language, Myth, and Custom." Through his discussion of Völkerpsychologie, Wundt decisively furthered
knowledge of the historical and sociological character of
religion.[6]

I have so far looked only at the humanities faculty and its
activity before 1912. At the theological faculty of those days,
by contrast, there were no lectures in the history of religions,
with one exception. The lecturer (Privatdozent) David
Johann Heinrich Goldhorn announced a course on "The Gen-

eral History of Religions" in the winter semester of 1837–1838. Unfortunately, I have been unable to discover any details of what he taught, for the theological faculty's archives have been almost completely destroyed.

Only toward the end of the nineteenth century was the strongly orthodox theological tradition at Leipzig first broken. At that time Franz Delitzsch (1813–1890) made Leipzig one of the leading centers for Old Testament and rabbinic studies.[7] The university's strong Lutheran faculty attracted the sons of Lutheran pastors in Germany.[8] The number of significant theologians who began their teaching careers at Leipzig in the 1870s and 1880s is astounding: Wolf Graf Baudissin, H. F. Mühlau, Emil Kautzsch, Bernhard Stade, Heinrich Guthe, Rudolf Kittel, E. V. Ryssel, F. E. König, Friedrich Loofs, C. R. Gregory, Friedrich Georg Heinrici, Adolf Harnack, Viktor Schultze, and Gustav Dalman. Significantly, some of the later leading scholars of the *Religionsgeschichtliche Schule,* such as A. Eichhorn, W. Wrede, and H. Hackmann, studied in Leipzig. A. Harnack, who taught in Leipzig from 1874 to 1879, was the central figure of the younger generation in Leipzig who left the orthodox Lutheran tradition. His first course on *Dogmengeschichte* (the history of dogma) was given at Leipzig in the summer term of 1877.

Alfred Jeremias (1864–1935) was the first to make the general history of religions an enduring part of the theological curriculum. Beginning in 1906, he lectured comprehensively on the history of religions. He taught as a lecturer (*Privatdozent*) for fifteen years before being promoted in 1921 to the position of associate professor of the history of religions, especially of Semitic religions. In his own day Jeremias was controversial as a historian of religions. He was a leading spokesman for "Pan-Babylonianism" and the theory of astral-mythology that accompanied it. With ever-increasing vigor, his works expressed his excesses and idiosyncrasies, but one should not overlook his merits. Jeremias can be seen as a precursor of those historians of religions who examine "patterns" and as the first to make profitable use of "motif-research" (he called it *Symbol-Forschung*) in the comparative study of religions. C. M. Edsman has considered him a sort of spiritual father to the modern notion of sacred kingship.[9] And through energetic use of cuneiform inscriptions, Jeremias and his colleagues freed the Old Testament from an unhistorical isolation and opened it up to historical interpretation.

Although his training was strongly philological, Jeremias himself was also concerned with the theological significance of his investigations. Besides teaching at the University, he served as a Lutheran pastor in Leipzig. For him, the history of religions confirmed what his own religious experience had convinced him of in practice, the absolute position of Christianity.[10] Thus, he conceived the history of religions in theological terms, trying to insure the objectivity of his statements through an inappropriate separation of feeling and expression.

During the period of Jeremias's activity, the department (*Seminar*) and the chair for the history of religions were founded in 1912, a turning point in the teaching of the history of religions.[11] The *Religionsgeschichtliches Seminar*—to use its old name—was located in the Institute for the History of Culture, founded by the historian Karl Lamprecht. Despite the established tradition of religio-historical research in the humanities faculty, the new institute was affiliated with the faculty of theology for "practical reasons," it was said. The Institute for the History of Religions was to supplement the work of the departments of Old and New Testament through its work on the religions of the ancient Near East and late antiquity. It is only to be expected that the humanities faculty, with its long history of pursuing religio-historical studies, would object to the appointing of a professor of the history of religions in the faculty of theology, but its protests were to no avail. A professor from the humanities did, however, serve as adviser to the department, and the purpose of the department's work was never said to be apologetic or theological.

The first to occupy the new chair and the first director of the new department was the Swede Nathan Söderblom. Because Söderblom returned to Uppsala in 1914 to become archbishop of the Swedish Lutheran Church, he actually worked in Leipzig for only three semesters. Nonetheless, his time there was significant. He wrote two of his best-known works, *Das Werden des Gottesglaubens* and an article, "Natürliche Theologie und allgemeine Religionsgeschichte" (Natural theology and the general, historical study of religions) while at Leipzig.[12] For Söderblom, the history of religions was theological, a new sort of "natural theology." As his Gifford lectures, *The Living God: Basal Forms of Personal Religion* (1931, published 1933), taught very clearly, the history of religions, in his view, served Christian apologetics. Owing to his short stay, Söderblom left only two pupils in Leipzig. One of his first assistants was a Japanese scholar, Jomonoba Ishibashi. The other student, H. W. Schomerus, worked as a missionary of the Leipzig mission in South India from 1902 to 1912 and translated religious texts from Tamil. In 1926 he became professor of missiology at Halle (Saale), Germany.

Söderblom's successor in the professorial chair was Hans Haas, an East Asian specialist. Haas assumed the position in 1915, and for the next twenty years his contribution to the history of religions—both at Leipzig and worldwide—was very great.[13] Among other activities, he compiled the first *Bilderatlas zur Religionsgeschichte*, which appeared in twenty fascicles from 1924 to 1934; he edited with Edward Lehmann the well-known *Textbuch zur Religionsgeschichte*, the first of its kind in German (1910; second, enlarged edition, 1924), and, from 1910 to 1931, he edited the *Zeitschrift für Mis-*

sionskunde und Religionswissenschaft. Haas's teaching was confined, for the most part, to his area of specialization. He did no more than touch upon the general problems of the discipline, and in opposition to the Marburg school, he avoided raising philosophical or theological questions.

Theologically, Haas was a liberal Protestant. He belonged to the General Evangelical Protestant Mission Union, later known as the "East Asian Mission." For him, the history of religions was, as P. de Lagarde has said, "a corrective to the customary, dogmatic activity of theology." Haas manifested this attitude in his works, Idee und Ideal der Feindesliebe in der ausserchristlichen Welt (The Idea and Ideal of the love of one's enemy in the non-Christian world) and Rechte und schlechte Apologetik in der allgemeinen Religionswissenschaft (Proper and improper apologetics in the general history of religons).[14] It is no wonder, then, that in a memorandum from the year 1927 Haas noted that his department would be better located in the humanities than in the theological faculty. Shortly before his death, Haas actually considered transferring his chair to the humanities faculty, despite opposition from church officials.

One of Haas's colleagues in the faculty of theology at that time, Johannes Leipoldt (1880–1965), was also strongly oriented toward the history of religions. Leipoldt's knowledge of the religions of late antiquity was extensive. In 1922 he published in Berlin a little-known Handbuch der Religionswissenschaft, which was never completed. He also founded a journal for the history and culture of the New Testament, Angelos (1925–1932). In addition to Haas and Leipoldt, I might also mention that Paul Tillich held an honorary professorship in the theological faculty from 1927 to 1929 besides teaching in Dresden at the Technical University.

During the early years of the history of religions in the theological faculty, religio-historical work in the humanities faculty did not stop. The achievements of a number of scholars were of decisive importance for the progress of research into specific religions. I think here of scholars like Johannes Hertel and Friedrich Weller, the Orientalist Richard Hartmann, the Sinologist Eduard Erkes, the Egyptologist Hermann Kees, the Assyriologist Benno Landsberger, the Arabic scholar Erich Bräunlich, Lazar Gulkowitsch, a rabbinic specialist, and the classical philologist August Körte, as well as such Germanic scholars as Helmut de Boor, Julius Schwietering, and Konstantin Reichardt.

But the most important event pertaining to the history of religions in the humanities faculty at the time was the appointment of Joachim Wach in 1924 as the first lecturer *(Dozent)* in *Religionswissenschaft*. Wach's appointment was in the Institute for the History of Culture and Universal History *(Institut für Kultur- und Universalgeschichte)*. He had studied with Friedrich Heiler in Munich and Ernst Troeltsch in Berlin, but his most important training had been at Leipzig under Hans Haas, August Fischer, Heinrich Zimmern, Hans Freyer, and Johannes Volkelt. Wach graduated from Leipzig in 1922 after writing a thesis on "The Foundations of a Phenomenology of the Concept of Salvation."[15] In 1927 he taught on the sociology of religion, a subject he was to advance significantly. Two years later he was named associate professor for the history of religions. But Wach's promising career was cut short in 1935 when Nazi barbarians revoked his teaching license, along with the licenses of several others. Some of the faculty protested this disgraceful action, among the most vehement being the mathematician Bartel van der Waerden, the physicists Friedrich Hund and Werner Heisenberg, and the archeologist Bernhard Schweitzer,[16] but protests were unsuccessful. At the time Wach had accepted an invitation to deliver a set of guest lectures at Brown University in Providence, Rhode Island, and the United States became his second home. From Brown he was appointed professor of the history of religions at the Divinity School of The University of Chicago.

There is no need to belabor the details of Wach's work and significance at Chicago. A few points will suffice. Wach's *Habilitationsschrift*, entitled *Religionswissenschaft* (Leipzig, 1924), laid theoretical and methodological foundations for the rather young discipline. In it Wach stressed particularly the independence of the history of religions from both theology and philosophy, although he himself did not always clearly maintain the distinction in his later writings. Ultimately, Wach belonged to the tradition of liberal theology, received from Ernst Troeltsch and Hans Haas. His methodology, influenced by the thought of Wilhelm Dilthey, runs the risk of irrationalism and shows a disregard for historical-critical studies. His orientation toward religious experience has its weaknesses, too. It is too closely tied up with the religious subject and it slides over and over again into theologizing or psychologizing. Despite my criticisms, however, Wach's writings on the comparative study of religions and the sociology of religions are still among the best. Wach was especially masterful in handling typology.

The vacancy created by Wach's forced departure was soon filled. In 1935 Friedrich Rudolf Lehmann's teaching license was broadened to include the history of religions as well as ethnology. In 1937 he was named associate professor in both areas. Lehmann's reputation had been established by two works, a dissertation on the concept of *mana* among South Sea Islanders, written in 1915 and published in 1922, and a comprehensive book on *tabu* customs among Polynesian peoples, published in 1930.[17] Lehmann was particularly concerned with problems of religious ethnology. Characteristic of his work is the care he exercised in confronting theories with facts. Even today historians of religion do not ponder his results sufficiently. Especially the badly out-of-date concept of *mana*, falsely applied in the dynamistic theory of religion, still appears in widely circulated publications. Lehman also opposed an excessive, one-sided stress on religious feeling in the history of religions and tried to turn attention back to religious concepts.[18]

In 1939, Lehmann's activity in Leipzig was interrupted by World War II. He was engaged in research in Africa at the time, and as a result he was interned in Pretoria. After the war Lehmann became professor of ethnology at Potchefstroom, South Africa, a position he held until 1965. He died in Munich in 1969.

Let me now turn back from the humanities faculty to the faculty of theology and its chair in the history of religions. After Haas's death in 1934, several problems surrounded the selection of a successor. Pressure exerted by the German Faith Movement (*Deutsche Glaubensbewegung*), which the Nazis promoted, caused a great deal of confusion. In the end, however, the faculty won the battle over the appointment, and Walter Baetke became the new professor of the history of religions. As Horst Stephan, dean at the time, remarked, Baetke's appointment preserved the "Leipzig chair's strong tradition of scientific methodology." Baetke was a first-class Germanic philologist. He also possessed a detailed knowledge of the rich world of religions. Especially significant was his opposition to the German and Aryan worship staged by the German Faith Movement's new heathenism in accord with the national-socialist *Mythos*. He was in an ideal position to explain to young theologians the Nazis' falsification of German antiquity. He clashed repeatedly with the regime in power, but he worked undeterred until the Nazi collapse, thereby contributing to making the young immune to the poison of the Nazi errors.

Like Haas before him, Baetke concentrated chiefly on his area of specialization. His election as the first Leipzig historian of religions to belong to the Saxon Academy of Sciences was due above all to his merit as a Germanic specialist. In all of his critical investigations of sources, however, Baetke never lost sight of religio-historical questions. His critical work on the Old Norse Sagas began with the question of whether and to what extent the traditional sources for the history of Germanic religion could be used generally as evidence for the pre-Christian period.

Within the history of religions itself, Baetke struggled persistently against drawing religio-philosophical and theological meanings from the discipline's materials. He continued the best tradition of German religio-historical research with its strong emphasis on philological and historical investigation. As I have tried to show, this tradtition has old roots at Leipzig. Of particular consequence was his opposition to Rudolf Otto, as seen in the introduction to Baetke's book, *Das Heilige im Germanischen* (The holy among the German peoples).[19]

Baetke's chief objections to Otto's fundamentally theological conception of the holy were two: it lacked any appreciation for the communal character of religion, and it was onesidedly subjective and psychological. Otto's notion began, falsely, with experience and feeling, and its goal was to comprehend the numinous or the divine empirically.

In Baetke's view the central elements of religion were the community, the tradition, and the cultus in which an individual's faith is rooted. Because Baetke emphasized the objective, sociological aspects of religions, he could not begin his interpretations of religions with "primal experience," a "movement of the numinous," or any similar category. The *history* of religions (*Religionsgeschichte*) does not begin with some primal experience of the numinous but with historical religions, to the extent that they can be recovered by an investigation of the written sources. Thus, Baetke avoided postulating any nonreligious origin for religion and any unhistorical evolution connected with such a view. He wanted to preserve intact the *historical*, empirical nature of the history of religions and to keep it far removed from any tendency to discuss philosophical, metaphysical, and theological questions.

Baetke sought fundamentally to eliminate from the history of religions the search for the origins that Friedrich Schleiermacher had initiated, and as a consequence sought to avoid the influence of theology and the philosophy of religion, particularly metaphysics, which had exerted its influence with disastrous consequences from the time of Schleiermacher to the time of Rudolf Otto.

To quote Baetke, "A history of religions which attempts to conceive of religion through the feelings and dispositions of its adherents, through their religious aptitude or through the kind of religious experience they have, and which as a result neglects the objective aspects of their faith, builds in the clouds."[20] Consequently, Baetke avoided Otto's notion of the holy. For him the holy was an objective concept, bound to a community and its traditions. Apart from these two it could not be understood. What is holy is determined not by the individual but by the community, or rather by the community's tradition. Baetke constantly stressed the central role of the cultus. In his view, the religious community is at the same time a cultic community. Therefore, one can speak of religion only in connection with a living cultus and faith. In fact, the *religious* significance of a myth depends upon its relation to cultus. Thus, Baetke strongly separated religion and mythology. Even today that separation is often forgotten or not sufficiently taken into account.

Furthermore, Baetke repeatedly stressed the close relations between religion, on the one hand, and *ethos* or custom, on the other. Something holy or numinous that lacks an aspect of custom was, for him, "merely imaginary, without any real foundation." "The holy," he said, "always has an ethical, obligatory aspect; otherwise it is only a glorified spook."[21]

Baetke obtained these insights, and others that comple-
ment them, from the study of the history of religions, not
from speculation or theory. In this he had much in common
with such scholars as Geo Widengren, Carl Martin Edsman,
Erland Ehnmark, Helmer Ringgren, Haralds Biezais, Ugo
Bianchi, Paul Radin, and others. In my opinion, Baetke was
influenced by Emile Durkheim, whom he quoted with ap-
proval.[22] He dealt seriously with the historical and sociological character of religions, and he strove to construct a history
of religions that was actually independent of theology and
the philosophy of religion.

The Institute for the History of Religions was destroyed by
bombing in 1943. After the war, Baetke undertook to rebuild
it. In 1946 he transferred the chair and department of the history of religions to the humanities faculty. Until 1959 he
served as professor of Norse Philology in the Department of
Germanic Languages in addition to working in the Institute
for the History of Religions. He died in 1978 at the age of
ninety-four. A host of important specialists worked with
him, specialists whom he had enlisted to share in the
teaching of the history of religions. Siegfried Morenz began to
teach Egyptian and Hellenistic religions at Leipzig in 1946.
Until his early death in 1970, he regularly gave courses as
professor of Egyptology on the history of religions. In addition to Morenz and Albrecht Alt, Baetke, and Leipoldt, several representatives of the older generation took part in rebuild-
ing the history of religions program at Leipzig: Eduard Erkes
(a Sinologist), Wilhelm Schubart (a papyrologist), Johannes
Schubert (a specialist on Tibet and Mongolia), Eva Lips (an
ethnologist), and Ernst Dammann (an Africanist who worked
at Leipzig as a visiting professor). From the Marxist side, the
historian Ernst Werner maintained constant contact with the
history of religions.

The years following World War II saw two crises in the
development of the history of religions at Leipzig. The first

occurred in 1958 in the wake of the second, so-called social-ist, reform of the university. At that time there was an at-tempt to turn the Institute for the History of Religions into an Institute for Atheistic Research and Propaganda. Baetke and Morenz both successfully opposed the attempt. The question of atheism's correctness is not a historical problem. Pro-paganda is not science's task. And, as Baetke said, "the histo-ry of religions can only fulfill its task if it is conducted as a historical science."[23] Because of this resistance, the Insti-tute's teaching was limited to students of theology, and its in-fluence generally declined. It no longer seemed likely that the Institute would expand, for expansion would have been possible only if the Institute had met the demand for atheistic research.

The second crisis occurred in 1968–1969, in connection with a university reform that profoundly altered university structures all over Europe. In the process, a dispute arose about where the history of religions should be located, whether it belonged to Oriental studies, history, or theology. In the end, the discipline was relegated to the historical division, and a chair was established on September 1, 1969. I was appointed to this chair after turning down a position at the University of Göttingen. The old Institute or Department for the History of Religions was abolished, as were all the remaining institutes, and the independent libraries were dis-solved, an act that did nothing to promote scholarly work.

Such has been the history of the history of religions at the University of Leipzig from the end of the eighteenth century to the present. This tradition has, I think, two fundamental characteristics.

First, it sees the history of religions or *Religionswis-senschaft* as a philological and historical study. Second, it sees the history of religions as proceeding inductively, as Wach set forth in his original program and as his student Joseph Kitagawa has continued to promote at Chicago. Emile

Durkheim had already said of the study of religions: "History is indeed the only method of explanatory analysis which can be applied to them." And Karl Meuli once said, "Questions in the history of religions are matters for the philologists."[24] He meant, of course, philology in the sense of a study of culture, a notion of philology promoted by August Boeckh and, later, by Ulrich von Wilamowitz-Moellendorff. Hermann Usener first put this concept to profitable use in the history of religions, and his pupil Albrecht Dieterich set it forth programmatically at the second congress for the general history of religions in Basel in 1904.[25] Shirley Jackson Case, too, had this study of culture in mind when he wrote the important lead article for the first issue of the *Journal of Religion* (founded in 1921) on "The Historical Study of Religion."

LECTURE
TWO

The Structure and
Purpose of the History
of Religions:
Its Role in the
Humanities

The history of religions, like so many neighboring disciplines, is a child of the Enlightenment. Curiosity aroused by the discovery of exotic cultures and the fight against religious intolerance assisted at its birth. Thus, the two countries most developed economically in the seventeenth and eighteenth centuries, England and the Netherlands, were pioneers in the history of religions, too. Ever since, the history of religions has displayed these two roots, scientific curiosity and religious tolerance, and it has been the fate of the discipline to be swayed back and forth between two poles, one theological or philosophical, the other philological and historical. Leading advocates of the young discipline during the nineteenth and twentieth centuries illustrate my point. As an Indologist and a comparative philologist, Friedrich Max Müller claimed to have laid empirical and inductive foundations for a comparative mythology and science of religion. But he also undertook to demonstrate his own philosophical and theological conceptions of general revelation and of the perception of the Infinite as the essence of religion. He did not make a sharp distinction between scientific evidence and theological convictions held on the basis of faith.[1] The Dutchman C. P. Tiele also fused the history of religions with the philosophy of religion. He took more account of ethnological, sociological, and psychological research than Max Müller had, but on the whole he sought a "natural theology" and did not clearly separate the history of religions from theology.[2] Similar comments could easily be made about the views of Nathan Söderblom.

But not all research in the history of religions at the time of Max Müller, Tiele, and Söderblom suffered from this confusion. Almost without exception, research that did not confuse history and philosophy or theology was found outside the field of the professional history of religions, that is, among philologists and ethnologists. Recall, for example, the ethnologists Edward Burnett Tylor and James George Frazer and the so-called ethnological philologists, for example, Hermann Usener, Albrecht Dieterich, Wilhelm Mannhardt, Wilhelm Roscher, Richard Wünsch, and Edmund Hardy. These scholars showed little or no dependence on theological conceptions. They were, to be sure, dependent on the contemporary ethnological theories that characterize their accounts: animism, totemism, magic, and so on. But the influence of theories and hypotheses is closely connected with the development of any science, particularly with the development of a historical science: it determines that science's progress. Theories are falsified through philological and historical investigation of the data—and a remarkable number of theories in the history of religions have succumbed to this process. But the weight and influence of theological, religio-philosophical, and metaphysical concepts are completely different. They strongly endanger the historical and philological character of the history of religions.

The situation of the history of religions in universities reflects its hybrid character. In Germany, the discipline has most often found a home in faculties of theology, and, for the most part, it has been theologians who have studied the history of religions professionally. Like Wilhelm Bousset, Rudolf Otto, Friedrich Heiler, and Gustav Mensching, they have often introduced their own religious and theological convictions into their work, especially theological concepts inherited from Schleiermacher, which emphasize a kind of psychological consciousness of God. My own thought has given much attention to the hybrid character of the history of religions in the recent past.

In 1888, Max Müller remarked on the study of the history of religions in Germany: "In Germany lectures on the great religions of the world were generally given by the professor who taught the languages in which the sacred writings were composed. This is an excellent plan, perhaps the best that could be devised."[3] But fully implementing a philological approach to the history of religions has its problems, as philologists themselves know best. The famous church historian at the University of Berlin, Adolf van Harnack, first brought the problems surrounding the history of religions as an academic subject to official attention in a rectoral address, "Die Aufgabe der theologischen Fakultäten und die allgemeine Religionsgeschichte" (The task of theology faculties and the general history of religions), delivered on August 3, 1901.[4] From this and from other writings we can isolate his three major comments on the pursuit of the history of religions: (1) the *general* history of religions runs a great risk of dilettantism; (2) the history of religions is best pursued by specialists, and consequently, it is best located in a humanities faculty; (3) the history of religions can exist in a faculty of theology only as a theological discipline.

I shall not address the third point directly here. From the standpoint of theology, it is easy to understand. It helps to draw clearly the boundaries between a nontheological, a pseudo-theological, and a theological history of religions. But the other two points are of immediate concern, and I shall take up each in turn.

In his time, Alfred Bertholet had tried to lessen the impact of the danger of dilettantism by alluding to the fact that the other humanistic disciplines, such as linguistics and the study of literature, face the same danger.[5] The point is, of course, true, but extensive translations from the pens of first-class specialists can help alleviate the risk to a large extent. Still, Harnack's admonition calls us to exercise a healthy caution. It emphasizes the demand that the historian of religions devote himself to a special field of research. The Orientalist Hans Heinrich Schaeder spoke to this effect when he said:

> I cannot conceive how a general history of religions can be called scientific today, how it can consider itself research. It may be an auxiliary activity for the researcher. It may stimulate and educate him generally. But in itself it is not research. Elevating it to independent status would produce the same result as elevating any form of dilettantism to independent status. It would demoralize the historian. It would place a burdensome demand on his conscience to do something that lacks the propriety and the significance of a proper undertaking.[6]

Schaeder welcomes—indeed, he demands—"philologizing" as a direction in which research in the history of religions must move. Joachim Wach, too, once remarked quite correctly that the historian of religions is never well enough equipped philologically.[7]

Harnack's second contention—that the history of religions is best placed among the specialties of the humanities faculty—is the appropriate and necessary consequence of his remarks on dilettantism. Only by placing the history of religions in that faculty which, in Europe, houses philological and historical studies is the historical and scientific pursuit of the history of religions assured. (Universities in the United States, of course, are organized differently. Apart from those colleges and universities that are clearly affiliated with a church body, American universities have no theology faculties in the European sense. They have only Divinity Schools, whose character is generally that of religious studies departments.) Moreover, we should not forget to include in the history of religions the study of the Old and New Testaments, even when it is placed in faculties of theology. Inasmuch as this study is strongly oriented toward the historical and philological sciences, its model is the type of work done in faculties of the humanities.

The organization of the *Ecole pratique des Hautes Etudes* in Paris is, actually, a model that I would recommend. Here the history of religions is the task of different branches of study—ethnology, Eastern and Near Eastern studies, the study of late antiquity, and so on. This arrangement conforms best to the character of the discipline as, to use Carsten Colpe's words, "a field of study whose boundary lines are displaced from time to time and occasionally even blurred."[8] But given the conditions in most universities, perhaps the best that can be done is for the professor of the history of religions to represent officially the interests of the discipline and to coordinate various courses relating to it.

So far, I have limited myself to general comments on the history of religions. Now I must set forth my conception of the discipline in detail. Of course, I am not the first to make such an attempt. One of the most reasonable is an essay by the Indologist Edmund Hardy, "Was ist Religionswissenschaft?," which appeared in the first volume of the *Archiv für Religionswissenschaft*.[9] This essay states very

clearly that the history of religions is a special human science
built of necessity on historical and empirical foundations.
Another good treatment is Joachim Wach's *Habilitationsschrift*, which provides a "theoretical grounding" for
the discipline. Published in Leipzig in 1924, the work carries
the programmatic title, *Religionswissenschaft. Prolegomena
zu ihrer wissenschaftstheoretischen Grundlegung*. From
more recent times, Walter Baetke's synopsis, *Aufgabe und
Struktur der Religionswissenschaft* (The task and structure of
the history of religions), conceives in exemplary fashion the
foundations of a history of religions independent of theology.[10] This conception is also found in the articles "Religionswissenschaft" and "Religionsgeschichte" by W. Holsten in
the third edition of *Die Religion in Geschichte und Gegenwart*.

In essentials, my view corresponds to that sketched by
Wach in the work just mentioned. For me, the history of religions denotes a discipline in the sense that it is *the* science
(*Wissenschaft*) whose object of study is the multiplicity of
religions, past and present. Religions appear historically and
sociologically. Therefore, we must investigate them historically and, in order to deal with the historical sources,
philologically (with the provision that "philologically" does
not mean linguistically!). As did Albrecht Dieterich, who
followed the lead of Ulrich von Wilamowitz-Moellendorf, I
use the term "philology" in a broad sense to denote the
scholarly investigation of a people's culture—in this case a
people's religion—on the basis of its sources.[11] The sources
for studying a religion are historical, "even," as Nicolai Hartmann said, "in those cases where faith perceives the content
of its teaching to be beyond history."[12] Thus, the history of
religions is a historical, not a philosophical or theological,
discipline. It is a twig from the bough of the history of culture
or, to use another image, a sister of the study of art, literature,
language, and music. It holds fast to its place in the universe

of the human or social sciences by reason of its specific object of study: religions as they appear in human history, or rather, in the history of human societies. No other discipline can ever deprive it of the investigation of that object. I will return to this topic in Lecture Three.

The history of religions must investigate its object in two ways. First, it must investigate and portray religions in their historical development, or, as Wach said, "longitudinally." This task is the task of what I shall call here "the historical study of religions" (in German, *Religionsgeschichte*). Second, the history of religions uses the comparative method common to all historical sciences in order to comprehend its object, so to speak, cross-sectionally, an undertaking that Wach denoted "systematic." To avoid misunderstanding, I must stress that the comparative undertaking proceeds from a historical basis. Its work is empirical, not speculative. A solid historical basis will prevent the systematic study of religions from slipping into theological or religio-philosophical speculation. As Wach said: "Inasmuch as the systematic study of the history of religions is an empirical discipline, it possesses no normative character."[13]

To my mind, the so-called phenomenology of religion is identical with the comparative study of religions. It occupies itself with religious phenomena in their systematic aspects. For example, it investigates the laws and development patterns pertaining to religious structures. It was Gerardus van der Leeuw who first made the phenomenology of religion a theological discipline, more exactly, a *theologia naturalis*. Wach was correct when he demanded "a clean, methodical separation of the historical and systematic [studies of religion]." To speak generally and comprehensively, the history of religions concerns itself with the "becoming" of its object through historical study and with the "being" of its object through systematic study, whether the latter is conceived as comparative or phenomenological. Of historical and systematic study Wach correctly states, "The division of the general history of religions into historical and systematic studies is exhaustive. Beside these two there is no religio-historical discipline."[14]

One could try, to be sure, to divide the historical study of religion into a "general" study concerned with the development of religion as a whole and "special studies" concerned with portions selected from the more general field, such as the religion of the so-called primitives. But the concept "religion" in the singular is much too general and hypothetical. It is heavily loaded philosophically and theologically, and in general it is not useful to the historian. For this reason I have in the past deliberately avoided speaking of religion in the singular, and I will continue to do so. Another method often talked about is the typology of religions, still very much in its infancy. But typology is not an alternative to historical and systematic studies. Rather, it belongs to the systematic study of religions, and like systematic studies in general, it is dependent upon historical research.

There are, of course, scholars who engage in a study of religions that is not history of religions in either its historical or its systematic aspect. Let us look at several of these other pursuits and the subject of supplementary or auxiliary disciplines in general. Actually, looked at from differing points of view, any discipline can become an auxiliary discipline for another.[15] Thus, both the sociology and the psychology of religions are auxiliary disciplines for the history of religions. They are specific sciences that apply their questions and methods to the object of the history of religions. Consequently, they deepen and promote the historian of religions' work.

The psychology of religions proceeds empirically. It is in part grounded in the natural sciences. Because the psychology of religions works empirically and experimentally, it pertains, strictly speaking, to the scholarly study of present-day religions. If it considers religions of the past, it must investigate them along the lines of the *verstehende* methodology developed by Dilthey. The psychology of religions runs the risk of concentrating too narrowly on the religious subject and hence of furthering a subjective, individualistic notion of religion. It seems to me that the danger of a one-sided subjectivism is best avoided by taking account of both the *Völkerpsychologie* developed by Wilhelm Wundt and modern social psychology. In this connection I quote Max Horkheimer: "Religion acquires all its content from the psychological processing of worldly events, but in the process it gains its own shape *(Gestalt)*, a shape that acts in turn upon psychical *(seelisch)* capability and human destiny to form a unique *(eigentümlich)* factor that influences social development as a whole."[16] In the United States, a psychology of religions has from the time of William James been oriented strongly toward the empirical and social-psychological investigation of present-day religions. A new approach to the psychology of religions has been provided by the application of "role psychology" to certain religious phenomena, as done by the ground-breaking work of the Swedish psychologist of religion Hjalmar Sundén. Sundén's psychology has been able, as a result, to do away with the old, outmoded concept of the "soul."[17]

The sociology of religions derived its initial impetus from the work of Karl Marx and Friedrich Engels. As is well-known, it was advanced by Max Weber, Ernst Troeltsch, and Joachim Wach, although the contributions of William Robertson Smith and Emile Durkheim should not be forgotten. Smith, and then Durkheim, made the most significant attempts to emphasize the social aspect of religion and gave religious research sociological depth. Durkheim understood the different levels of society as the means through which a concept, for example, *mana*, was received.[18] Except in the case of a few excesses, his work has still not been surpassed.

"Orthodox" Marxist analysis, however, follows the theories
of nature-mythology and animism more than it follows
sociological and historical theories.

Work in the sociology of religions continues to yield prof-
its, but research on the local level—the community, the
parish, the church—has been more fruitful than consideration of universal aspects, which was done in such an exemplary fashion by Max Weber. Modern experimental methods
have cast much light on the contemporary religious situation in several fields. In fact, the method of the history of
religions—the historical method—is of necessity closely
connected with the method of sociology. The historian of
religions cannot investigate and describe the forms in which
religions appear without considering communal development. As Marx once said, a pure history of ideas leads to a
"ghost-history."[19] Each religion is bound to a community.
More than any others, categories from the sociology of
religions—categories such as community, cultus, founder,
and sect—make the description of religious phenomena,
strictly speaking, possible at all.

In the United States, the scientific study of religions is
identified mostly with the sociology of religion, as in A. W.
Eister's *Changing Perspectives in the Scientific Study of
Religion* (New York, 1974) or Milton Yinger's well-known
Scientific Study of Religion (New York, 1970). Such a one-
sided emphasis gives a distorted image of the history of
religions, but it can be significant for that discipline—particularly for its social-scientific side—as a means of keeping
speculation, theology, and philosophy in check.

On this point the German historian Richard van Dülmen
has written:

Religion is unthinkable apart from the social activity
of humanity and its community. Consequently, religion can only be conceived in the context of the
sociological formations in which it is found or in
which it acquires social and political significance. If

the history of religions proceeds with a view of the essence of humanity provided by religion, it can only treat religious phenomena in a religious sense, that is, as holy and numinous. But so conceived it cannot deal with the social role and character of religion, or with its central function as a means of orienting persons in a given community toward the world. Historical research on religion thematizes religion as a social phenomenon and analyzes it against the background of the social interests of the groups that bear it.[20]

One of the disciplines that have assisted the historian of religions the longest is the ethnology of religions. Ethnology has contributed such well-known theories of religion as animism, totemism, and dynamism (that is, the *mana* theory). By contrast, one of the youngest of the auxiliary disciplines is a branch of geography, the geography of belief systems. In recent times this discipline has grown enormously, especially through the work of Manfred Büttner at Bochum.[21] Büttner's work expands the older beginnings of a geography of religions by incorporating questions of a social-geographical nature. In doing so, it portrays and thematizes the dialectical relations between a religion and its environment. Landscapes have been formed and destroyed by religion. Cityscapes and landscapes that are completely traditional can be understood only by referring to correlative religious traditions—churches in Christian countries, mosques in Islamic countries, stupas in Buddhist countries. In this way, it is possible to see that religions are constants in space and time.

The philosophy of religion can include many enterprises: analytical-critical realism, as in the work of Nicolai Hartmann; speech-analysis, as in the work of Ludwig Wittgenstein; the stark empiricism of Rudolf Carnap; Marxism; and many others. But the questions philosophy asks always transcend the given object and lead to general statements that, we can safely say, have the character of principles. In every case, philosophy lays claim to validity (*Gültigkeit*), as, for example, in Carnap's conceptual analysis and Wittgenstein's language analysis, both of which are otherwise especially useful to the historian of religions engaged in formulating concepts and questions. The history of religions and the philosophy of religion can learn from each other, but on principle, work in the philosophy of religion is not research in the history of religions. Therefore, I exclude the philosophy of religion from the domain of the history of religions.[22]

The differences between the history of religions and the philosophy of religion can be illustrated by considering the concept of "religion" itself. More than any other discipline it is the philosophy of religion that would discuss the concept "religion" in the singular. For the historian of religions there is, strictly speaking, no "religion" at all. There are only religions. Religion in the singular is an abstraction of metaphysics or theology, inherited from the age of Rationalism, from German Idealism and Romanticism. I think here especially of Hegel and Schleiermacher. Thus, "religion" in the singular is a loaded term, and any historian who adopts it without testing is thereby dependent upon a philosophical or theological theory. Historians of religions should be especially careful to avoid the duality of "essence" and "manifestation" presupposed by idealistic Hegelianism. Instead, they should speak of facts (*Sachverhalte*), traditions, ideas, cults, and rituals. Strictly speaking, then, there is no history of religion; there is only a history of religions and their eventual interrelations, or a history of religion in a particular cultural area, at a particular economic or social level, and so on. The history of religions acquires knowledge of religion only through a historical study of religions. I will take up the difficult problem of how a concept of "religion" can be obtained from historical and systematic studies in Lecture Three, and the problems surrounding a consideration of the development of religions in Lecture Five.

A discussion of the philosophy of religion leads almost inevitably to the vexing problem of the relation between the history of religions and theology. I began this lecture by mentioning the hybrid character which the history of religions has often assumed. On the one hand, it has inclined to theology or the philosophy of religion; on the other, it has veered toward history, and to philology in particular. A glance at the proceedings of recent international congresses for the history of religions is sufficient to show that the hybrid character is still present in current work. A particularly influential and harmful tradition that confuses the history of religions and theology has developed in Germany.

This unfortunate development—which broke with the solid German tradition of historical and philological investigation—began with the famous Marburg theologian Rudolf Otto (1869–1937). Otto advocated the history of religions as a means of grasping the numinous by analyzing religious feeling.[23] The apparent but merely external scientific trappings of Otto's works, especially of his well-known book *Das Heilige* (first edition, 1917), cannot hide the fact that he assigns to the history of religions the task of a *theologia naturalis*. The concept of "the numinous" functions for Otto and his pupils as a sort of proof for the existence of God built on psychological grounds. In addition to the influence of Schleiermacher and neo-Friesianism, this conception derives largely from Otto's own strong inclination toward mysticism. Otto himself valued theological contemplation more highly than mere knowledge about religion, and with his concept of divination, he introduced into the history of religions a form of the Christian teaching on the Holy Spirit. Thus, Otto undermined the historical, scientific character of the history of religions and transformed the discipline into a pseudo-theology and psychology of religion. His irrational, subjective, and individualistic conception of religion is not acceptable to a strict history of religions. Neither is his focus

on the *Urerlebnis* (primal religious experience), which leads
to an ahistoricism that characterizes this entire approach (up
to Mircea Eliade). Although Otto's influence has hurt more
than it has helped the independent status of the history of
religions, he was strongly opposed by only one German historian of religion, my teacher in Leipzig, Walter Baetke.

Of those scholars who carried on Otto's work, two were
especially prominent, Gerardus van der Leeuw (1890–1950)
and Friedrich Heiler (1892–1967). Van der Leeuw's
Religionsphänomenologie, translated into English as
Religion in Essence and Manifestation, is impressive for the
massive amount of material it contains. Nonetheless, it is
theological at heart.[24] The volume appeared in the "Neuen
Theologischen Grundrissen" edited by Rudolf Bultmann,
and to my mind van der Leeuw leaves no doubt that his work
was done in a theological context. He conceives the phenomenology of religion as a kind of philosophy of religion or natural theology. At the center of his analysis stands an "ex-
periential understanding." "This experience," he says, "is
more an art than a science." "Phenomenology is not a
carefully reasoned method but the proper activity of human
life." Understanding turns "chaotic and inflexible reality
into a manifestation, a revelation."[25] Van der Leeuw supposes that *epoché*, bracketing oneself in the presence of that
which appears, will prevent the phenomenology of religion
from becoming metaphysics. Questions on van der Leeuw's
conception of *epoché* aside, he himself does not really exercise it. By scientific means he tries to gain information about
that which stands behind religious phenomena; that is, he
tries in the end to gain information about God. When, for example, I read his section on "Religion" (section 110), I have
no doubt that here we have the confession of a modern Christian seeking God.

Friedrich Heiler takes up a similar set of problems as part
of the history of religions in his last great work,

Erscheinungsformen und Wesen der Religion, but his treatment is not so eccentric as van der Leeuw's. For Heiler, too, phenomenology serves to prove God's existence. In his view, religion is the worship of mystery and submission to it; it is "intimacy with the Holy." On the basis of the testimony of the German mystics Heinrich Seuse and Thomas à Kempis, Heiler asserts, "Man does not seek God; God seeks man." And in more detail, he says, "In essence, religion is the communion of men with transcendent reality which results from the experience of divine grace, a communion that attains fullness in adoration and sacrifice and which leads to the sanctification of men and humanity."[26] Heiler's work remains a rich source of religio-historical materials, but these few quotes clearly demonstrate that Heiler advocates a theological history of religions or a "religio-historical theology."

The same is true of Gustav Mensching (1901–1978), one of Rudolf Otto's students. Mensching maintains, "Religion is life, not rational contemplation or ritual. Therefore, it is something irrational, which one cannot approach if one relies totally on precise empirical methods of research. . . . The transparency of the phenomena, in which—as the name itself says—a Something 'appears,' must be taken into account. In this way religion is understood from within, from life; in this way inner necessity is recognized from outer manifestations." This "Something" of which Mensching speaks is apparently the "Numinous," God as the ultimate reality.[27] In Mensching's view, the history of religions should be a methodical means to a knowledge of this "Something."

I mention here only one other advocate of this train of thought, Joachim Wach (1898–1955). In the latter part of his stay at Leipzig and more fully during his career in America, Wach abandoned his original aim of developing a history of religions independent of theology and the philosophy of religion and allowed a place to questions that are obviously theological.[28] Especially the lectures published posthu-

mously under the title *The Comparative Study of Religion*
(New York, 1958) manifest this characteristic. Wach bor-
rowed from the psychology of religion in America the notion
of religious experience *(Erfahrung)*. At times he employed it
typologically and phenomenologically, but at times he used
it to make theological statements, that is, statements of faith,
and he did not distinguish theological statements clearly
from statements appropriate to the history of religions.
Wach also spoke of "revelation" and "ultimate reality," and
in doing so, he actually advocated a theory of general revelation. Like the notions of religious experience *(Erlebnis)*
held by Otto, van der Leeuw, Heiler, and Mensching,
Wach's notion of religious experience *(Erfahrung)* is theological. It deliberately avoids Otto's orientation toward the
psychological and the emotional; but still, subjective and individualistic factors are prominent, and as a result, Wach's
notion is not at all suited for work in the history of
religions.

Otto, van der Leeuw, Heiler, Mensching, Wach—all essentially sacrificed the historical, scientific character of the
history of religions to theology. Future historians of religions
must recognize this danger and seek to overcome it. They
must clarify the boundaries between their discipline and
theology. They must even go so far as to exclude theological
terms grounded in faith—such as "revelation"—from their
vocabularies.[29] This is not to say that historians of religions
and theologians should have no contact with each other.
Because they share in part the same object of study, historians of religions and theologians can learn from one another.
Historians of religions must be familiar with statements
made by theologians in a particular religious tradition. They
must try to understand them in terms of historical and systematic or comparative questions. But they need do no more.
Historians of religions will, to be sure, have a certain prior
knowledge of the object of their research, but to the extent
that they have neither a positive nor a negative attitude

toward the object of their study, they will be without prejudice. It is in this sense that historians of religions must be objective, that they must be as neutral as possible.

It is pleasing to find a theologian such as Walter Holsten, who approves of the strict approach to the history of religions as conceived by Walter Baetke and myself. In Holsten's contribution to the *Festschrift* for Baetke, he sees the call for a genuinely independent history of religions as part of the struggle, common to historians of religions and theologians alike, against a "secret theology hiding itself behind the mask of the history of religions."[30] Both theology and the history of religions are concerned with historical humanity, theology with historical humanity as it is touched by revelation, the history of religions with the religious activities of historical humanity. If theology is to perform its task well, especially in a secularized world, it must have reliable, scientific information about the world, even about the world of religions, with which it can confront its own assertions. A history of religions behind which a crypto-theology or a pseudo-theology lurks cannot provide theology with the information that it needs about the world.

My brief summary cannot do justice to Holsten's notions and the notions of others, but I hope I have said enough to indicate that they are a real contribution to the discussion of the relations between theology and the history of religions. One can say that the history of religions does not actually touch the theological sphere of faith at all. It deals with the manifold historical expressions of a religion's faith, not with the truth which that faith may contain. Questions about religious truth (*Wahrheit*) and questions about a religion's reality (*Wirklichkeit*) must be kept separate. Questions of truth are the concern of philosophy or theology—even if that philosophy or theology happens to be atheistic. Questions about reality—and these include questions about meaning (*Sinn*)—can and must be posed by the history of religions.

The most precious possession of any science, including

the history of religions, is a healthy, sober positivism. The historian of religions can make no use of theology, because the system of references (*Bezugssystem*) that lies at the root of every theology reaches into the transcendent, that is, into the domain of faith. The historian of religions must be able to verify his results through valid, scientific methods. Even when his topic is a statement of faith, he treats it scientifically according to his own historical or systematic questions. His concern is with the documents of a faith's history, not with the transcendental objects of faith. For him there is, strictly speaking, no "holy"; there is only a scientific inquisitiveness, paired with respect and understanding, directed toward a religious tradition as the object of his research. In this way, the objectivity of a historian of religions' statement about religions is guaranteed.[31] This guarantee is welcome to the theologian as well as to the historian of religions, for what the theologian needs from the history of religions are results that are as objective and factual as possible, results that are not encumbered with crypto-theological or crypto-philosophical judgments.

A saying by Martin Buber illustrates my point of view well: "The science of religion detaches the relationship of the human to the divine as that alone which can be investigated by it, detaches this relationship from the reciprocity and observes it in itself. If this science knows what it does thereby, it acts legitimately, in the sense of the legitimacy of every striving for knowledge that does not overstep its normative limit but rather remains aware of this limit and allows its work to be codetermined by it."[32]

LECTURE
THREE

The Autonomy and Integrity of the History of Religions

Several signs indicate that the history of religions is experiencing a crisis. There is uncertainty about the discipline's proper object of research, expressed above all in the question of what religion really is. The widening gulf between the historical and the systematic or phenomenological approaches is leading to a veritable methodological dualism. Religio-historical work is becoming increasingly entangled with the work of various specialties, especially philological work in individual cultural areas, and this entanglement threatens to dismember and demolish the discipline. The history of religions also stands helpless in the face of the demands of the sociology of religion, just as it once stood helpless before the psychology of religion. Furthermore, historians of religions are being overwhelmed by the increasing flood of material available to them and by self-critical reflec-

tion on how to master it. Especially in the phenomenology of
religion there is an abysmal gap between what historians of
religions claim to be doing and what they actually do. As was
seen at the international congresses held in Tokyo (1958),
Marburg (1960), and Claremont (1972), historians of religions
display an increasing propensity to wander in directions that
are not scientific. As a result, the distinction between the history of religions, the philosophy of religion, and theology has
become blurred. Finally, the discipline is relatively poorly
represented in European institutions of higher learning, and
the number of historians of religions among the younger generation of scholars is rather small.

These and other signs of crisis invite us to reconsider the
fundamentals of our discipline. Has the history of religions
been for the past 150 years only a *fata morgana*, a mirage?
Has it drawn its life more from its claim and from its grandi-
ose program than from a reality that it aims to investigate, to
explain or understand, and to depict? Work already accomplished might seem to indicate otherwise, but it has not
been able to forestall signs of crisis. Quite the contrary, it has
had a hand in bringing them to the light of day.

If we examine the present situation carefully, we can detect in the current crisis two fundamental problems. First,
what is the status of the discipline's object? On the answer to
this question rests the discipline's autonomy and its ultimate
salvation from destruction or dissolution. Second, what is
the status of the discipline's methods? On the answer to this
question rests its integrity. Only by answering these two
questions can we establish the history of religions as an ex-
acting and independent scholarly pursuit and counter de-
structive criticism based on its uselessness and on its uncertain position in the universe of the human sciences. I will
take up each in turn.

What is the object of *Religionswissenschaft*? The customary answer is found in the designation itself: religion. On oc-

casion this simple answer has been criticized and set aside as only postponing the real problem. I myself have stated repeatedly—as I did in Lecture Two—that historical understanding knows of no religion (in the singular) but only religions. But my assertion, too, only defers solution of the problem. One must still explain what "religions" are. We come straight away, then, to the vexing problem of defining religion.

The older style of research sought to understand religion from its origin. It sought to grasp the essence of religion by going back to its embryonic form. All scholarly efforts of the nineteenth and the early twentieth centuries were dominated by this evolutionary mode of thought. To the extent that scholars placed in the foreground questions about religion, the history of religion, the development of religion, and so on—in each case using the term "religion" in the singular—they linked their questions from the very beginning with the question of the *essence* of religion. As Joachim Wach already stated clearly in his methodological *Prolegomena,* the question of the essence of religion is a matter for philosophy that has been foisted upon the history of religions from without.[1] Nevertheless, all religio-historical theories of the time sought to answer this question, and the answers that they believed they had found varied considerably. The names of these theories reveal the religious phenomena that each considered original or fundamental: fetishism, animism, preanimism, totemism, and so on. Of course, my observations are not new and, to some extent, they beat a dead horse, but, they are important for my theme, for when the quest for the essence of religion was abandoned, the history of religions lost an important pillar in the definition of its object.

The modes of investigation that arose in the following period—the historical, the psychological, and the sociological—did not meet with resounding success in determining the nature of religion, but one approach in particular did exercise a great deal of influence, the school founded by Rudolf Otto. By means of an intuitive, phenomenological, and psychological analysis of both the experiences peculiar to the religious subject and their literary manifestations, Otto's school arrived at a very convenient "minimal definition" of religion: religion as simply the "veneration of the Holy." Just as before, the history of religions was left with the task of determining what "the holy" might be and how it might be regarded as a specifically religious category. It is well-known that many things are holy today that were once profane, and vice versa. The "excursion" into the holy seems to me to have effaced the boundaries of the history of religions rather than to have marked them out more clearly. It led the history of religions too far again into the ambit of the philosophy of religion or theology. Behind Otto's "holy" lurks, admittedly, the Judaeo-Christian notion of God.

More recently, historians of religions have propounded similar "reductions" or "operational definitions" for religion, such as the operational definition advanced by the Japanese scholar Hideo Kishimoto or the "key word" that the Dutch scholar C. J. Bleeker hit upon.[2] But in general, as Richard van Dülmen laments, attempts by historians of religions to define religion have either been so distinctive—and as a result so exclusive—or else so formal and general that they have been of little use in historical work.[3]

The time has come, it would seem, to abandon such "brief definitions" or "key words" and follow instead the lead of Th. P. van Baaren. By working inductively, van Baaren lists, precisely and concretely and as exhaustively as possible, the characteristics that historians, ethnologists, philologists, and others have ascribed to religion in order to formulate a definition or circumscription with which they can work.[4] Ugo Bianchi has given attention to the preconditions that make it possible to formulate such a definition.[5] Leaving to one side all reductive and a priori definitions of religion, Bianchi sets in their place a dynamic, dialectical procedure. The researcher approaches his material with a certain "prior understanding" peculiar to himself. His work leads to a broadening of his experiences and to a correction of his notion, to a "posterior or subsequent understanding," as it were. Thus, without resorting to any a priori idea, it is possible to arrive at a positive and inductive definition of religion that does justice to the complexity of the object. The procedure is based on the analogical and comparable traits in individual religions and their elements. These traits lead to the establishment of common aspects or families of characteristics that are always in the process of becoming. It is based on the one hand on the investigation of an increasingly broader amount of material, and on the other on the researcher's prior understanding and its successive broadening through as comprehensive a historical understanding as possible. This "dialectic" of research, hypothesis, and knowledge is the only possible way to escape from the cul-de-sac that has until now blocked a solution to the problem and to include the problem of the definition of religion directly in the method of research.

To "circumscribe" (umschreiben) the troublesome object "religion" is not an easy task. Not only does the common lack of appreciation for the difficulty create problems, but each religion is a world unto itself. The continuities between religions are undeniable, but various religions cannot simply be related to one another directly and without further ado. As Bianchi says, it is necessary to remain conscious of the complexity and multiplicity of the historical facts and processes that we call "religious." Only the scholar who possesses a sufficient amount of experience and a rather large amount of historical knowledge is in a position to give positive, historical, and phenomenological content to the concepts "religious" and "religion."[6]

One feature common to the pre-understanding of all of us needs to be reckoned with: the Judaeo-Christian conception of religion, which, although altered, still determines and shapes our research. In the Enlightenment, the concept of religion was severed from its concrete, Christian foundations and directed in abstract form—deism, natural religion —against the official manifestation of the Christian religion. Even earlier, during the Reformation and the heyday of humanism, the notion of religion had assumed a strongly doctrinal connotation, for religion was identified with "pure doctrine," a proper belief in God. In these forebears of our modern term the original, Ciceronian notion of religion as the worship of the gods can hardly be recognized.[7] For the most part, our concept is much too narrowly bound up with doctrine and thought. Consequently, we must be wary of using the term "religion" without reflection, especially when dealing with cultures and traditions outside of Europe. Moreover, the prior understanding of religion derived from Christianity entangles us over and over again in theological nets. What we need, rather, is a religio-historical "net," if I may call it that, that circumscribes what "religion" is, or what "religious matters" (Sachverhalte) are, for the history of religions.

Th. P. van Baaren and the "Groningen Work Group" have recently emphasized that religion is strongly entangled with culture. In fact, most conceptions of religion used by modern ethnology, especially ethnology influenced by functionalism and structuralism, speak of religion solely in terms of culture. One cannot deny, of course, that religion and culture are closely interrelated. Nevertheless, the autonomy of religion should not be short-changed. The object of the historian of religions' study does not simply evaporate into its context. What is true of the human sciences in general must also be true for the history of religions: the object of its study is not first constituted by the transcendental stipulations of some methodology or other; rather, it has already been encountered as it is constituted.[8] But in what form has it been encountered? That, of course, is the problem.

At the end of much investigation, it is perhaps possible to define the scope of religion. I would say that religion is an umbrella term for the traditional belief of a community or of an individual in the influence of superhuman and supernatural powers of various sorts which affect natural and social occurrences, together with the resulting worship of those powers through specific actions which are handed down in fixed forms by the community and about which is grouped a set of doctrines, transmitted orally or in writing.[9] A definition of this sort encompasses the essentials, to be sure, but it does not include everything. It is only a heuristic device, a sort of "rule of thumb" for "in-house" use. It is equivalent to the "prior understanding" mentioned earlier, and it must be vindicated through further research.

For our fundamental problem, however, it is better to begin with encountering the specific appearances and expressions of the various religions as these can be seen and comprehended. We can then proceed from the external to the internal. We can begin with all visible, cultic actions and places where these occur, with the persons who celebrate them, with the specific forms of community we encounter, their functionaries, their sacred writings, laws, and songs. All of this is empirical evidence in the strictest sense of the word. Here even the most inveterate skeptic and opponent of a *Religionswissenschaft*, of a "science" directed toward religions, stumbles across what I might call the positive object of study, the sort of object with which proper sciences are correlated. It is the duty of the inquisitive mind and the methodically bridled investigative impulse to examine this object in a variety of ways, not only to describe it superficially but to *understand* it, to comprehend its meaning and to see how it is put together and how it has developed. Without

such an understanding of religions, human thought and behavior are not completely comprehensible.

The history of religions investigates a portion—and a very
extensive portion—of human history and culture. The legit-
imizing ground for the discipline's existence is that it does
not merely poke around here and there among religions but
investigates them in the manner of a special science according to the requirements of methodical investigation. It cannot
fully realize its claim. A sufficient number of institutions, investigators, and other prerequisites is lacking, and the ex-
panse of its object exceeds its present capabilities. Nevertheless, in the universe of the human or social sciences, the history of religions alone holds the proper and legitimate place
devoted to its object of study. Neither psychology nor sociology, philology, or ethnology can assume its task and make its
claims. Certainly there are specialists in these fields who con-
centrate on religious matters, just as the historian of religions
is active and should be active as a specialist in a particular
area. But even if the study of religions is indispensable if
these disciplines are to have a complete grasp of the objects
that they study, it is not their primary task but an incidental
one. It arises from the scholar's education, interests, and
research program, not from the conception that lies at the
heart of his or her discipline.

I might add that in practice these other disciplines, too,
are not so autonomous as they might appear. Their objects
are beset with difficult problems of definition—what precisely are language, society, art, literature, music, and so
on?—and they must have recourse to the assistance of other
disciplines. No human or social science can persist in
absolute autonomy or even absolute autarchy. If one tried, it
would work to its own destruction. This is even more true
today than it was in the past. Today the individual sciences,
particularly the historical sciences, are drawing closer
together. Every aspect of human culture can be investigated

historically. This investigation is the task of the general science of history, to which the history of religions and other
specialized disciplines belong.

A second pillar supports the history of religions, the effort
to establish its method, or rather, its methods. From the unmistakable autonomy and peculiar character of its object
arises the question of whether a peculiar method is appropriate and required for this study. Those who assert that it is
generally talk of an intuitive vision, sympathetic understanding, or the role of a divinatory faculty. Through difficult efforts, the history of religions has succeeded in freeing itself
from such approaches. Today it is only in narrowly theological or religio-philosophical circles that such terms as "em-
pathy" or "intuition" are generally heard.

If one proceeds from the assumption that it must be possible to understand the object of the history of religions scientifically, one must speak above all of its historical side.
Religions are encountered primarily as historical forms with
their various traditions and appearances. Erich Rothacker
has written: "Everything that living human beings—and we
know of no other—have actually known and will know of
ideals and values must of necessity be transformed into a
solitary historical phenomenon. This is due not only to their
spatial, temporal, and psychic realization in the thought of a
being inevitably localized in history. It is also due to their
very content."[10] Historical methods correspond to historical
forms. *Religionswissenschaft* is at heart a historical science; the historical study of religions forms its basis.[11] At the
center of its work stand religions and their various aspects as
they appear historically. Every aspect of religion that we
might study is subordinate to the historical. Thus, the history
of religions adopts the general historical method and its
various procedures as these have been developed from the
nineteenth century on. That the historical method itself has
its own problems to work out and is subject to continuing

methodological discussion does not alter its place in the history of religions. Rather, historians of religions should take a
more active part in discussions among historians.

When the historical method is adopted for the purposes of
the history of religions, the object of study requires that the
method be altered and broadened somewhat. Historians of
religions must deal with the psychological and sociological
sides of religions. For this they require the assistance of psychology and sociology, particularly social history. They also
require help for problems concerning the philological-historical and aesthetic aspects of religions. Therefore, historians of religions make use of a combination of methods as
they attempt to deal with their material. Such a combination
of methods is not unique to the history of religions, but it is
extremely deep-rooted there, because the roots of this discipline's methods lie in actual research work, not in a priori
speculation.

Now the area specialist, especially the philologist and the
ethnologist, will ask, "What distinguishes the historian of
religions from area specialists? After all, area specialists are
frequently concerned with religio-historical problems, and
they generally use the same methods as historians of
religions to solve them." To respond, we must direct our attention to another method that is native to the history of
religions, the comparative or systematic method, more particularly, the phenomenological method. Again, the object of
study has itself made this method necessary. The historian of
religions meets with connections, analogies, similarities, and
parallel processes that induce him to employ the comparative method in order to do full justice to his object. In this
area in particular lie the discipline's major theoretical
problems. The so-called comparative study of religions has
been subjected to a continuous critique from historians,
philologists, and other scholars.[12]

The first point to emphasize is that the use of the comparative method and the problems accompanying it are not peculiar to this discipline. In particular, the history of religions can profit much more than it has in the past from discussions in the field of general history. In history, the comparative method is a systematic, historical method that serves as an important heuristic means. It is directly concerned with working out types and structures, that is, it is interested in classifying and formulating general statements, but without becoming thereby a completely generalizing mode of thought. In history, comparison is understood above all as a means of formulating more precise distinctions. The German historian Theodor Schieder assigned to it two chief tasks: "First, the working out of historical individualities by confronting them with and distinguishing them from others; second, the construction of general concepts by a comparative survey of the individual historical forms in which they appear." He calls the first "individualizing comparison," the second "synthetic comparison."[13]

Schieder also formulated six rules to be observed in historical comparison, some of which deserve notice here. Schieder emphasized that the "unities of a higher order" formulated by synthetic comparison should not be identified with "ideal types," for the former are perceived throughout as historically real. He also stipulated that "the historical phenomena to be compared must in some way belong to integral units of meaning, such as cultural circles, social structures, epochs, states, and nations."[14] He explicitly excluded from such units of meaning morphologically affined groups such as are found in Spengler's and Toynbee's theories of culture. As Reinhard Wittram has written, "Comparisons are only possible when our overview is so broad and general that we perceive the fundamental characteristics of each situation."[15] As long ago as the first decades of the twentieth century, Georg Wissowa, the well-known historian of Roman religion, raised another issue important for comparative

work, an issue that historians of religions have too often ig-
nored. "Is 'religiosity,'" he asked, "really a completely set
concept, a concept constant for all times and places?" He
then continued, "If anyone supposes that the religions of the
Greeks, Romans, Indians and so on differ only so far as their
content, but that in other respects they permit or require the
same manner of treatment, he will come to understand them
only with difficulty."[16] If the history of religions is to be
seriously comparative, it must meet all of these conditions.

The primary use for the comparative method in the history of religions is in systematic study, for which comparison is
indispensable. The systematic study of religions, as Th. P.
van Baaren has masterfully conceived it, has only one fundamental task: to order the material by means of comparison,
to classify and "systematize" it, and in so doing to understand it more deeply. "Systematic" here is understood in the
sense of the systematic human sciences, which stand over
against the individual human sciences and which develop
general synopses and theories on the basis of social and historical life. One should not sharply separate systematic study
from historical study on the grounds that it works systemat-
ically and leaves empirical work behind. Rather, it is very
carefully developed from a historical field of research and
employs the comparative, historical method together with its
systematic and theoretical implications. To my mind, the difference between the systematic and the historical sciences is
only relative.[17] Neither can do without the other.

However the ultimate goal of systematic investigation be
defined—whether as the formulation of laws, or rules, or categories, or concepts, or types, or structures—that goal
cannot be reached apart from comparative and historical
methods. From the study of history we learn that all work
with types and structures is built upon historical study.
Types are "conceptual schemes that function heuristically
and hermeneutically."[18] They possess a quality of "translat-
ability."[19] Every type which the study of history has devel-

oped—synchronic types, developmental types, ideal types, real types, Gestalt types, and so on—has been developed from comparison except one, the unreflective "cryptotype," as it were, to which our term "religion" and a great many others belong. Similar comments can be made about "structures," which have been established as a kind of synchronic type. In the case of the history of religions, the discovery of a structure in the historical material provides a deeper knowledge of religious phenomena in their complexity and interconnectedness. The procedure would be unhistorical only if the structure were hypostasized in its apparently static condition or if it were granted absolute dominion over all other factors of historical life.[20] It remains for future research in the history of religions both to work out regional and universal typologies that do not lose themselves in insignificant games and to oppose research into religious structures or systems that denies the claims of historical study.

Until now I have deliberately avoided using the terms "phenomenology of religion" and "phenomenological method," because, as I noted in Lecture Two, they are problematical. Gerardus van der Leeuw, for example, was motivated, on the one hand, by concerns of theology and the philosophy of religion, and, on the other, by his close ties to Gestalt psychology and the phenomenological method of Husserl and Heidegger, to use a concept of phenomenology that was quite unusual in the history of religions. All subsequent phenomenologists of religion have sought either to diverge from him in fundamentals or to use the concept "phenomenology" in a way that is identical to the comparative or systematic study of religions. At the same time, voices have been raised questioning just how far phenomenology can really claim to be a method for the history of religions.[21] It seems to me that we have two options today: we can either preserve van der Leeuw's aims and methods, in which case we establish phenomenology in his sense as a third method beside the historical and the comparative, or we can use

"phenomenology of religion" as a more euphonious name for
the comparative study of religions, as has been done since
the time of Chantepie de la Saussaye. I prefer the second alternative for two reasons. First, with the exception of van der
Leeuw, phenomenology of religion is fundamentally systematic or comparative. Second, only by taking the second alternative can the unity of the history of religions be guaranteed.
By reintroducing the philosophy of religion, van der Leeuw's
phenomenology dynamites, as it were, the edifice of the history of religions. If one adopts Husserl's manner of working,
then one must occupy oneself with essences (Wesensschau);
one must consider the essential, reduce eidetically, and so
on, even if one would like to extricate oneself from all of
this.[22] Furthermore, the often deplored and lamented dichot-
omy between the phenomenology and the history of religions has its principal roots in van der Leeuw's work.[23]
Only by returning to the original goals of the comparative
study of religions can it be set aside.

   A glance at several recent practitioners of the phenomenology of religion will illustrate how some of the harmful effects of van der Leeuw's heritage are being overcome. Geo
Widengren has discussed "The comparative method between
philology and phenomenology."[24] For him, the phenomenology of religion is a systematic ordering and analysis of
meaning that does not violate historical facts and that
includes philology as an integral component. In Widengren's
view, philology and comparison are successive stages of
research. He outlines four steps coinciding with the procedure I have sketched: the description, the systematization,
and the interpretation of the facts, with the construction of a
type, a structure, or something similar as the fourth step. But
to my mind, the first three steps are often combined into the
single operation of philological and historical work. Only the
fourth step—comparison, typologizing, and so forth—stands
by itself.

   For Åke Hultkrantz, too, phenomenology is meaningful

only when accompanied by a "feel for the historical."[25] It has three tasks: to search for the forms and structures of religions and, in the end, religion; to attempt to understand religious phenomena; and to supply the history of religions with a meaning that makes it cohere as a discipline encompassing all religious forms. Hultkrantz emphasizes that the comparative study of religions, instead of beginning with the most general conclusions, should concern itself first with specific fields and cultural zones. Only the sort of regional phenomenology practiced by Hultkrantz, Ingmar Paulsen, and others can provide a solid basis from which to make universal comparisons. The manner in which Hultkrantz conceives phenomenology as working is also commensurate with my understanding. In his view phenomenology proceeds by taking an inventory, identifying, classifying, comparing, and systematizing.

Although C. J. Bleeker's conception of the phenomenology of religion resembles van der Leeuw's more closely than either Widengren's or Hultkrantz's views do, nevertheless Bleeker, too, explicates clearly the contributions of phenomenology to historical study.[26] Bleeker distinguishes four branches in the history of religions: historical study of religions, general historical study of religions, comparative study of religions, and phenomenology. In his view, phenomenology is "a systematization of historical facts in order to grasp their religious value."[27] Because comparison does not rest content with classifying but always leads to questions of meaning and deeper understanding, I cannot agree with Bleeker that the distinction between comparative study and phenomenology is fundamental. Bleeker assigns to phenomenology a threefold task—the investigation of the *theoria*, *logos*, and *entelecheia* of religious phenomena—but he does not specify the methods by which this task is to be accomplished. He notes five contributions that phenomenology can make to historical study, contributions that resemble some of Hultkrantz's notions: (1) clarification of

formulations and presuppositions; (2) sharpening of the view
of the specific nature of religion; (3) clarification of the meaning of religious phenomena; (4) insight into the essence and
structure of religious phenomena; and (5) clarification of the
concept of religion. Without historical inquiry, any attempt
to approach any of these points would evaporate into triviali-
ty.

What, then, distinguishes work in the history of religions,
particularly historical work, from parallel work by the
philologist and the area specialist? The distinctive contribution of the history of religions resides precisely in the greater
compass in which the historian of religions locates his
researches. It is this greater compass that secures for the historian of religions his right to be heard by the area and regional
specialists, provided his work is serious, scientific, and as
extensive as possible. The historian of religions should always be both a specialist in the history of a particular religion
and a comparativist or systematist. He is always interested in
seeing individualities in association, first regionally, then
globally. In this way he enriches and supplements the work
of philologists, ethnologists, sociologists, and regional historians. Almost every term used in religio-historical work leads
out of the sphere of the specialist's competence to universal
questions which only the historian of religions can and
should answer.[28] It is the complexity of the universal and
the specific, the global and the regional, and the intertwin-
ing of the synchronic and the diachronic that mark off the
history of religions from other approaches and demonstrate
its autonomy. In the final analysis, the object of study itself,
which cannot be mastered by an individual specialty confined to a religion, a culture, or a people, calls for a science
that encompasses and unites several methods of study. Such
a study portends a needed and promising corrective to the
increasing specialization of our age.

LECTURE
FOUR

The History of
Religions and the
Critique of Ideologies

In most of the so-called human or social sciences the "critique of ideologies" (*Ideologiekritik*) is a catchword that enjoys great popularity. The term was first developed in philosophy and sociology, and in recent years students of history, literature, linguistics, and art history have increasingly busied themselves with the task. Without a doubt, they have made important contributions to their fields. But the history of religions has been an exception. There are various reasons for its peculiar stance, reasons that derive from the discipline's history and methods. It is time, however, for the history of religions to concern itself seriously with the critique of ideologies. Not only is such a critique opportune from a scientific point of view; it also opens the possibility of directly addressing the political and social reality of our time.

I approach the topic in three stages. First, I discuss briefly the concepts of "ideology" and "the critique of ideologies" and their relation to "religion" and the "history of religions." Then follows an excursus into the history of the changing relations between the history of religions and the critique of ideologies, particularly the critique of religions. Finally, I outline the tasks of a critique of ideologies conducted by the history of religions together with its difficultues and practical consequences.

The word "ideology" is popular today, but the more it is used, the less is said about its history and meaning. The term arose in French (materialistic) sensualism of the late eighteenth century.[1] The Abbé Bonnot de Condillac (1735–1780) analyzed human consciousness as a permutation of meaningful perceptions. He found influential followers in the physiologist Cabanis (1757–1808) and Count Destutt de Tracy (1754–1836). These two were called "ideologues" because they considered the chief task of philosophy to be the psychological dissection of human concepts or ideas. In the five volumes of his Eléments d'idéologie (1801–1805), de Tracy dealt with the generation of ideas in a sensualistic sense. He became the father of "ideologism," a view in vogue in France throughout the nineteenth century. Because the "ideologues" derived practical rules for education, government, and law from their results, they came into conflict with those in power. No less a figure than Napoleon I spoke disdainfully of them, considering them nothing but mere theorists, ignorant of the world, whose ideas were only chimeras lacking in practical significance. Thus, from the very beginning "ideology" was stigmatized, and its negative connotations have remained up to the present time. In addition, the term has always been connected with praxis and politics.

I cannot pursue the history of the word "ideology" and its meaning in detail here. Karl Marx and Friedrich Engels took up the notion in its contemporary sense. Throughout their The German Ideology (composed in 1845–1846 but not published until 1932), "ideology" is used negatively to describe what at the time was—as the subtitle has it—"modern German philosophy according to its representatives Feuerbach, B. Bauer, and Stirner, and German Socialism according to its various prophets." But the word carries a more general meaning, ideology as one side of human history, a side that comprises a "twisted conception of history" or a "total abstraction from it."[2] Marx and Engels mean the conscious world of human concepts, and they demonstrate that this world takes its rise in concrete social, political, and economic conditions, even if it does not correspond to them precisely. At one point in the book they say in blatant opposition to Max Stirner:

> All these spectres which have filed before us were ideas. These ideas—leaving aside their real basis (which Stirner in any case leaves aside)—understood as ideas inside consciousness, as thoughts in people's heads transferred from their objectivity back into the subject, elevated from substance into self-consciousness, are—*whimsies* or *fixed ideas*.[3]

As used by the left-wing Hegelians, then, "ideology" is a view that sees (as Hegel did, too) ideas as the stimulating powers of history. It produces a ghost or phantom history, instead of a real history, a history that sees the empirical as the true foundation for the history of ideas.[4] A "real, positive science" must begin with the empirical. Thus, Marx and Engels gave "ideology" a new tone through their concrete, historical vision. In the subsequent periods their sense of the term became strikingly visible. Through the scientific sociology of the 1920s, it has been passed down to modern sociology.

In a letter to Franz Mehring dated July 14, 1893, Engels wrote briefly and to the point: "Ideology is a proces that takes place in the consciousness of the so-called thinker, but in a false consciousness. The real powers motivating him remain

unknown to him. Otherwise, the process would not be ideological."[5] From the standpoint of Marxism, "ideology" is especially the perverted consciousness which, governed as it is
by social relations, does not and cannot construct a proper
image of history. Only the correct, Marxist insight leads to a
proper historical consciousness and to an ideology that corresponds to the real motivating powers of history. According
to the contemporary Marxist conception, ideology is the specific sum of communal perceptions, to which belong philosophy, religion, music, and science, the so-called super-struc-
ture. It serves the interests of individual classes or of the
"communal consciousness" of the class powers.[6] Whether an
ideology is correct or false is determined by its place in the
class struggle, which also determines its contents. Thus,
ideology is functionally dependent, not absolute.

The non-Marxist concept of ideology, by contrast, is not
uniform. It ranges, so far as I can see, from a view close to that
of the Marxists' to a positivist conception such as that of
Theodor Geiger. For Geiger, ideology is the "not being-in-
harmony-with" reality. All metaphysical and theological assertions belong to ideology, since they pass their subjective
judgments of value off as objective assertions of descriptive
knowledge.[7] A German volume edited by Kurt Lenk makes
the disparity more than clear. The editor does not offer a definition of ideology, but he does describe various points of
view in a phenomenological, typological overview.[8]

If one wishes to use "ideology" in a neutral manner, that
is, as a scientific technical term, one must begin with the
word's root meaning and use it to denote "the teaching of the
science of ideas." But such a meaning is unhistorical. It ig-
nores the almost 200 years during which the term has been
used and debated. It seems better to me to use "ideology" for
human concepts as they are constituted historically and
stamped with a particular worldview and as they decisively
determine human thoughts, perceptions, and behavior.[9] The

variety that is thereby brought together into an invisible, abstract concept is useful only when employed in the service of concrete historical or philosophical work. It, too, will have to engage in self-critical reflection, to see whether it has itself been inherited ideologically.[10]

To what extent can what is usually designated "religion" be subsumed under the concept "ideology"? (For the sake of expedience, I will violate history here and use the term "religion" in the singular.) "Religion" is frequently so subsumed, and as a result the history of religions is at times dissolved into a history of ideologies.[11] But actually religion can only partially be classifed under ideology. Its past and present forms embrace more than ideas. One encounters in individual religions and religious forms much that falls outside the scope of ideology: the entire cultus and social organization, for example, except insofar as these are given their characteristic shape by ideas. Certain manifestations are quite clearly defined by a religious ideology. The Christian church, particularly in its Roman Catholic form, and the community of traditional Lamaism are cases in point. But this religious ideology is only one side of religion. The other side includes praxis and cultus, ethics, and social organization. For the time being we can say that religion consists both of an "ideology"—a religious ideology or the ideology of a religion—and of a social, political, and moral praxis.

The almost constant companion of the term ideology is the critique of ideologies. My brief overview of the concept's history has already given a taste of its critical function, particularly in my discussion of the Marxists' use of the term. In a Marxist context, "ideology" cannot be used in a neutral sense. The critical evaluation of the dominant ideology that was carried out by Marx and Engels has influenced the term's meaning decisively. The "ideological class struggle" is an essential form of the debate with the "bourgeois ideology." It does not cease even under the sign of "peaceful coexistence." It only becomes a more peaceful struggle, a struggle with weapons of the mind.

The non-Marxist conception of "the critique of ideologies," like the non-Marxist conception of "ideology," is quite diverse. Of course, it can in general be designated a "bourgeois critique of ideologies," but otherwise, one can only refer to critiques of ideologies of various kinds. Geiger has spoken of two sorts of ideological criticism, a "pragmatic critique of ideologies," a critique that is not dependent upon science, and a "theoretical or logical critique of ideologies," a critique that seeks to expose failings of thought as a scientific program.[12] I, too, have made it a practice to distinguish different sorts of ideological criticism: philosophical, sociological, historical, and political or pragmatic. No sharp line separates these four. They are dependent on one another and refer to one another, so that they can and often do intermingle.

The history of religions can be combined best with two sorts of ideological criticism, the sociological and especially the historical critique of ideologies. These connections do not, of course, preclude the possible significance of a philosophical or pragmatic critique for the history of religions, but in general, because the history of religions understands itself primarily as a historical and philological discipline, it is closest to a critique of ideologies of the historical sort, that is, a factual critique striving for objectivity that arises out of historical work as such. It includes criticism of sources and traditions as well as the critical reflection about the world of religious conceptions, together with that reflection's emancipating consequences, to which a criticism of sources and traditions gives rise.

In addition to the critique of ideologies, one can also speak of a critique of religions per se. Where ideology and religion overlap, their critique is a common enterprise, dedicated to the same object. But, as I have stated, religion and ideology are not identical. Consequently, it is also necessary to distinguish two sorts of criticism. The critique of religions is a critique of ideologies that relates to a religious ideology or to the ideology of one or several religions. The four sorts of ideological criticism that I have distinguished can also help differentiate the critique of religions in a narrow sense from the critique of ideologies. A pragmatic critique of ideologies, that is, a critique that seeks to destroy religion from political motives, cannot be the task of the history of religions. But insofar as sociological and historical critiques can be beneficial to religio-historical activity, they have every right to a place within the discipline. Thus, the critique of religions is dependent upon and defined by its fundamental purposes and methods. But while the history of religions benefits from ideological-critical undertakings and from religio-critical deliberations, these critiques do not constitute its primary task. For the history of religions, the critique of religions arises as a result of the ideological criticism that it pursues, implicitly but also explicitly, as a historical and philological discipline.

The extent to which it is advisable for the history of religions to engage in the critique of ideologies is shown by reflections that attempt to mediate between the "scientific" and the "hermeneutical," or between "explanation" as practiced by the natural sciences and "understanding" as sought by the human sciences. The history of religions is often cited as an example of a human science that employs only the hermeneutical concept of *Verstehen* (understanding) developed by Wilhelm Dilthey and his school. Men like Gustav Mensching have spoken of a history of religions oriented toward understanding as the discipline's crowning task and method.[13] Today we can see more clearly than in the past the danger associated with the "pure *Verstehen*" position. This form of hermeneutics has been opposed by critics who appeal to a neo-positivistic model of explanation developed in the Anglo-American theory of science. They conceive of understanding as a preparatory psychological reconnaissance of the territory on the part of the individual who engages in scientific explanation. That is, they conceive of understanding in terms of a knowledge of causes and effects and the laws that govern their operation. The onesidedly hermeneutical model of understanding has caused investigators to neglect the criticism of traditions and the criticism of the history of historical effects (*Wirkungsgeschichte*), and that neglect now requires the corrective of analytical and critical rationalism.

Working from opposite sides, Hans Albert and Karl-Otto Apel have attempted to bridge the gap between understanding and explanation in order to provide a firm and methodologically sound foundation for historical knowledge. Both have assigned a significant place to the critique of ideologies. For Albert the significance of ideological criticism lies in furthering clarification, scientific, anti-dogmatic thought, and freedom from prejudice.[14] For Apel its significance lies in abolishing the unreasoning aspects of our historical being, that is, in removing that which is irrational by nature. Apel conceives of this activity as a sort of "'Psychoanalysis' applied to the history of human society" and a "'Psychotherapy' applied to the actual crises of human activity." In his view, it presents the only meaningful, logical foundation and moral justification for human sciences that are objective and pursue explanation.[15] Hans-Georg Gadamer, too, allows hermeneutical reflection to become ideological-critical. "It makes every ideology suspect," he writes, "because it makes one conscious of pre-judgments."[16] Thus, hermeneutics and the critique of ideologies interpenetrate. From these concerns of the philosophy of history, the history of religions, too, can derive its right to incorporate the critique of ideologies into its investigations.

Thus, we discover that the actual ideological-critical function of the history of religions derives from its object and its character. As I have set forth in Lecture Three, the history of religions is an objective, philological-historical, and comparative-systematic discipline of the human sciences that is not bound to any religious worldview or judgment. Strictly speaking, it knows of no "holy" as such that it could master by extending its tools. Its scientific ideal, which includes a "methodical atheism" or "methodological agnosticism," is really already ideological-critical.[17] It brackets the claim to value that religious assertions make in the context of their own traditions and it does not and cannot take seriously that claim's existential reference. If it did, it would dissolve into a plurality of religious confessions. Scientific distance with respect to its object of study—which, of course, does not by any means require a lack of interest—places the history of religions from the beginning in an ideological-critical or rather a religio-critical position. The discipline divests religions of their claim to truth, authority, and divine revelation and analyzes them on the dissecting tables of history, sociology, and psychology. Thus, the history of religions is a particularly clear example of how a scientific and critical procedure presumes, or rather, implies, an ideological-critical consciousness. The scientific method dispels the luster of the supernatural halo, of the epiphany of the divine, of "ultimate reality" from this field of knowledge and activity, a field that humanity finds so deep existentially. To the extent that the history of religions is a scientific endeavor, it exercises a critical function.

To be sure, a "critical consciousness" is not foreign to religions themselves. The critique of religion can be performed within a religious context. Richard Schaeffler has investigated the critique of religion from within religion in his book, *Religion und kritisches Bewusstsein.*[18] For Schaeffler, the opposition between a critical consciousness and religious consciousness is not absolute. Religion, too, contains a "critical consciousness." I cannot agree completely with all of

Schaeffler's views and conclusions, both philosophical and historical. Still, he does demonstrate a close connection—he calls it a correlation—between religion and criticism. As a result, religion is relevant to the self-understanding of critical consciousness. On the one hand, a religious form of critical consciousness stands beside the philosophical form. It is older than the philosophical and prepared the way for it. On the other hand, the critique of religions is a religious as well as a philosophical concern. Schaeffler thus points to a phenomenon in religious history that he calls "religio-critical religions."[19] For support he cites the "religious revolution" of Akhenaton, the mystery cults, and Zarathustra. Christianity is included in the list too. It prepared the way for the modern critical, secular consciousness and, in fact, gave birth to it.[20]

But Schaeffler overlooks the fact that what he calls an "innerreligious critique" is often introduced into a religion from the outside and should not always be treated as religiously autonomous. Moreover, the so-called religio-critical religions must be taken with a grain of salt. They are specific religious forms that arise from ordinary religious traditions and seek to overcome them. Actually, what we are talking about here is the spirit that moves prophets and reformers. In the background lurks the really astounding phenomenon that, through the agency of individuals and groups, religions— above all, "religions of the book"—can raise self-critical questions. All the great world religions were born from just such acts.

The origins of the religio-critical religions should not be thought of as "purely" religious. They are, in fact, multiple, but they may be understood under the sign of religion. The theological tradition has repeatedly laid claim—as did Luther and Calvin—to the right to self-criticism. Hans-Joachim Kraus, for example, has evinced a critical stance from the Barthian point of view in his latest work.[21] To quote

Dieter Rössler, "Religion is in itself critical of itself. It criticizes its own principles on the basis of reality; and it critically examines the difference between what its principles say it should be and the way it actually appears."[22]

From the self-critical procedures of the various religions the history of religions can infer that critical activity is not alien to its object. On this score it is possible for a historian of religions who is also an adherent of a particular religion to further his field's task in critiquing religions and ideologies through his own critical, religious consciousness. There is no reason to view religious consciousness, insofar as it is self-critical, as an obstacle to objective historical and cultural work in the history of religions. The history of religions arose from the Christian tradition, even if it often opposed it, and it has taken its critical presuppositions from that tradition.

Before turning to the varied past relations between the history of religions and the critique of ideologies, I would like to mention a form of ideological criticism from which the history of religions can learn a great deal, the ideological-critical investigations of Ernst Topitsch. Topitsch's analyses of the mythological, metaphysical worldview, from its primitive origins to its after-effects in the modern conception of the world, have an effect that is directly ideological-critical. They demonstrate that these structures depend upon prehistoric experiences. Concepts modeled on biological, human, technological, and sociological forms are, for the most part, patterns whose characteristics derive from our traditional religious, philosophical, political, and aesthetic worldviews and from the way that we, as human beings, have understood ourselves. The mechanism of projection that appears here under the influence of Feuerbach and Freud has direct consequences for the history of religions. The religio-mythical tradition played an essential role in the formation, transmission, and reception of worldview. It was transmitted for reasons of psychological, practical, and political expediency, not because it was correct. Only thus can we explain why this particular view of the world was considered valid for thousands of years.[23] The normative model, a model that derives the effectiveness of this worldview from the surface intentions of those who held it, produces only empty formulas (*Leerformeln*), which precisely because they are empty, can be applied universally.[24] In his work Topitsch shows clearly how an ideological-critical illumination of tradition can be of direct relevance to our present view of man and the world. "Scientific knowledge," Topitsch remarks, "must deny fulfillment to many desires. It can proffer no consolation and no feeling of security. It must, in the end, reveal for what it is the subtle act of self-illusion that has been and still is practiced with the help of empty formulations."[25]

Despite the promise of the critique of ideologies for the history of religions, relations between the two have varied considerably. The origins of the modern history of religions lie in the critique of religion, above all, the critique of organized Christianity, in the seventeenth and eighteenth centuries. Two concepts played leading roles in the development of this critique: the theory of priestly fraud and the notion of the so-called natural religion. The idea of a religion innate in man was first directed against the *ancien régime* and the church in prerevolutionary France. Thus, it was of direct political significance. Attempts were made to provide both notions with foundations from material offered by the history of religions, especially from Picart's great work, *Cérémonies et coutumes religieuses de tous les peuples du monde* (Amsterdam, 1723–1728). The critique of tradition found in Picart's work was often incorporated directly into the critique of religion.

The first historians of religions—men like Christoph Meiners, Johann Friedrich Kleuker, and Christian Wilhelm Flügge—were content to work empirically, with an eye to the

historical sources. They also strove to overcome the overwhelming power of Christian dogma in order to establish an
unbiased treatment of religion that did not prescribe its
results prior to its investigations and that found truth, not
merely error and paganism, in other religions.[26] In this struggle, Johann Gottfried Herder's influence was decisive. Following him, Schleiermacher formulated a widely influential
notion of religion as a natural human capacity that has value
even outside Christianity. Here the heritage of the Enlightenment was combined with a theological, romantic spirit. To be
sure, the eighteenth century's emancipating interest in
religion did not carry through to the end a direct critique of
religion or of ideology. But the critique did enter, in altered
guise, the common notion of religion, which became increasingly opposed to the theological and dogmatic conception.[27]

In the nineteenth century the religio-critical spirit, now
informed by Hegelian dialectics, was represented by Ludwig
Feuerbach. On the whole, Feuerbach's effect was limited to
the philosophical critique of religion, especially the critique
advanced by Marxism. One can hardly detect any impact of
his thought on the young discipline of the history of
religions. So far as the philosophy of religion was concerned,
the history of religions was nurtured on the heritage of
Herder and Schleiermacher. It did not realize that it was
precisely that conception of religion—the religion of the
heart, of the soul, of sentiment—with which Feuerbach
began his entire critique. Neither Feuerbach's ideological-critical tendency nor his anthropological point of view influenced the history of religions, but the young discipline did
maintain a critical function by virtue of its tolerance, its uni-
versality (as evidenced in its concern with comparison), and
its general concepts of religion and of God.

The impulse to construct a history of religions as an autonomous discipline standing next to the other human sciences rather than as a mere division of theology or the philoso-

phy of religion is visible especially in the work of Friedrich
Max Müller. The new science gained an unexpected mastery
over the field of religious history through the historical-
philological method. This critical procedure flourished first
in the study of non-Christian religions, but it was applied to
Christianity, too, under the banner of the *religionsgeschichtliche Schule*. In the process its critical ambitions
were transformed into an ideological-critical tendency.
Christianity was seen as a particular form without absolute
character.

If ethnology and philology dominated the history of
religions in the nineteenth century, in the twentieth their
preeminent position has passed to psychology and sociology.
An even stronger spirit critical of religion and ideology has
resulted, but now the tenor is not pragmatic, as in the eighteenth century, but, naturally, psychological and sociological.
Although the ideological-critical debates of the twentieth
century have only recently begun to affect the efforts of the
history of religions, they can be of decisive importance for
the discipline's self-understanding and relative autonomy.
By reclaiming a critical attitude toward religious traditions
and interpretations and by setting aside prejudices, ideological criticism can help free the history of religions from the
clutches of theology and missiology. To the present day the
history of religions has repeatedly served, directly and indi-
rectly, the self-establishment of Christianity or the justification and furthering of an aspiring "religion of all humanity."
Only thanks to the guiding lights and the overwhelming ma-
jority of the members of the International Association for the
History of Religions have the most recent world congresses of
this body avoided slipping into congresses of religion after
the model of the Parliament held in Chicago in 1893. If the
history of religions is to preserve its present spirit and further
its autonomy, it must not only work out the peculiarities of
its methods, it must also revive its religio-critical, or rather,
its ideological-critical function.

There are five areas in which the history of religions may critique ideologies effectively. First, it may engage in the criticism of traditions, an implicit part of all religio-historical investigations. Criticism of traditions should be pursued more actively than it has been in the past and with a greater awareness of its contribution to the critique of ideologies.

Second, the practice of critiquing traditions would have an enlightening and emancipating effect on the self-understanding of contemporary religions, which are still in part rigidly orthodox and dogmatic. As Gadamer has stated, "To the essence of historical sciences belong the interpenetration of critical explanation, which criticizes the naive respect for traditions, and the traditions, which continue to be effective and which help determine the historical horizon." The component of reflection implicit in religio-historical work should not be underestimated in the formation and furthering of critical thought. To quote Rüdiger Bubner, "When reflection is prepared for by a critique of ideologies, the concrete, historical character (Signatur) becomes transparent to the object of reflection." Dilthey, too, wrote, "Historical consciousness breaks the last chains which philosophy and the natural sciences have not been able to destroy."[28]

Third, the history of religions should investigate critically the changing entanglement of religion and politics, "church" and "state," especially in regard to the various religious ideologies of dominance that have left religion open to manipulation.[29]

Fourth, the history of religions should pursue and attempt to validate historically Marx's notion of religions as, on the one hand, "the opium of the people," and on the other, "the protest against real distress."[30] In doing so it will acquire insight into the meaning and use of religious concepts—the relation between religion and economics, between religion and the social structure, and between apocalyptic, eschatology, and the expectation of salvation.

Fifth, the history of religions should broaden its scope to

include pseudo-religious, crypto-religious, and para-
religious movements, the "religious underground of our
world." With the help of religio-historical methods and the
knowledge they provide, these movements can not only be
explained in historical and traditional terms, they can be understood as an expression of a worldwide resurgence of a
suppressed natural religiosity.[31]

From these five areas of ideological criticism the history
of religions provides its work with a new dimension, but it
also acquires a great responsibility, especially to the Third
World, which is in the midst of a far-reaching process of
emancipation extending even to its own traditions. Apel was
correct when he wrote:

> The direct, dogmatic and normative application of the
> understanding of tradition, established institutionally
> and socially obligatory, functioned within Europe
> until the Enlightenment and in most cultures outside
> Europe up to the present time. Now, however, it can
> no longer be revived. . . . By being alienated inevitably
> from their own traditions, the third-world cultures tes-
> tify that systems of meaning—for example, religious
> and moral orders of value—must be conceived in
> closest connection with the forms and institutions of
> social life. Above all, they seek a philosophical and
> scientific orientation that mediates the hermeneutical
> understanding of their own and of foreign traditions of
> meaning through sociological analyses of the respec-
> tive economic and social orders. This more than any-
> thing else makes it easy to understand the power
> Marxism has to fascinate intellectuals of developing
> countries.[32]

The history of religions can help Third World peoples obtain a new, critical, reflective relationship to traditions that
have a strong religious character. To quote Apel once more,

"As soon as it has become possible to objectivise and distance the meaning to be understood from normative values, even if only provisionally, through hermeneutical abstraction, the mediation of a tradition must become a complex process facilitated by scientific scholarship."[33]

In my opinion, the destruction of mutual prejudices and misconceptions is possible only through the critical relativizing of religious confessions and traditions that is brought about by religio-historical work. To this degree, a critique based on the history of religions—a historical, philological, sociological, and psychological critique—posseses an altogether positive significance for the common life of humanity. It furthers understanding, tolerance, and mutual recognition on the ground of a shared approach to a tradition that is not accepted without examination. "Culture and science can liberate humanity from its natural, uncultivated environment as well as from its enslavery to its own irrationality."[34]

Development as a
Problem for the
History of Religions

Whoever is familiar with the older, general surveys of religious history, particularly those of the nineteenth century, knows the great and apparently uninterrupted role played by the notion of a more or less direct development or evolution of religion from its primitive beginnings to the spiritual heights of the world religions, particularly Christianity. The prevalence of evolutionary views resulted above all from the working out of the theory of biological and anthropological evolution, that is, "evolutionism" in the narrow sense. In this regard, the greatest influence on the history of religions was Edward Burnett Tylor. For an entire generation, and probably longer, ethnologists and historians of religions worked in Tylor's shadow. Tylor himself expressed the dominant frame of mind concisely: the "growth" of human thought from its primitive, simple beginnings as, he supposed, these could

still be studied among modern-day primitives, to the heights
of contemporary science and philosophy "may bear comparison with one of the great changes in the mental life of the individual man, perhaps rather with the expansion and fixing
of the mind which accompanies the passage from infancy
into youth, than with the later steps from youth into
manhood, or from manhood into old age."[1] Just as ontogeny
and phylogeny were set parallel to one another in biology, so
too were human biological development and world history.[2]

An instructive and typical example of the use and modifi-
cation of evolutionary ideas in the study of religion is the
work of C. P. Tiele, one of the founders of the history of
religions. Tiele's "Grundzüge der Religionswissenschaft"
(Fundamentals of the history of religions) presents a brief introduction to the discipline.[3] Towards its beginning, Tiele
writes on "The Concept of the Evolution of Religion." He
explicitly employs here the biological theory of pre-formation, according to which the steps of evolution are already
contained in the seed—the oak in the acorn, the adult in the
child. In reference to religion he states: "Religious evolution
is an internal process, the development of the religious consciousness and disposition. It is the work of the human mind
(Geist), which strives to discover an appropriate and ade-
quate expression for religious ideas that become increasingly
clearer." Tiele often combines idealism and biologism. He
sees each stage of religion as striving to clarify, purify, deep-
en, and elevate the religious consciousness. He divides
religions into two major groups, "natural religions" and
"ethical religions," each of which is subdivided in terms of a
developmental sequence. In addition to this "vertical development," Tiele also distinguishes "horizontal development"
in terms of religious families. Every religion, in his view, and
many individuals as well, have contributed in their own
ways to the general religious development (pp. 21–24).

The laws according to which evolution proceeds are not,

in Tiele's view, either laws of nature or historical laws. Rather, he concludes: "If one supposes that there are no special laws governing religious evolution, that is correct insofar as it is not religion but, strictly speaking, the religious man who evolves. Accordingly, one can only speak of the laws that the evolution of the human mind follows, and in our case we apply these laws to religion" (p. 25). Such laws include the unity of the human mind, the law of development through mental interchange and assimilation, the law of continuity or of concentration and expansion, and the law of equilibrium and synthesis. Despite the rise, blossoming, and decline of individual religions and religious forms, religion itself continues to evolve further without ceasing. The peculiar and essential evolution of religion consists in the continuous purification of religion from nonreligious elements through which it becomes both more self-sufficient and internally stronger. According to Tiele, two groups of factors combine to set this process in motion: unconscious factors, such as the "tendency toward differentiation" and the "tendency toward unification and association", and conscious factors, that is, individuals with particular religious capabilities, whether teachers, preachers, reformers, or founders (pp. 30–32).

Thus, in Tiele's view there are fundamentally two "evolutions" in religion, one of the surface features or external "husk"—that is, of religions or religious forms—and another of the internal, the kernel, that is, of religion in general. The latter is an evolution of the religious mind, or rather, of human consciousness.

The major characteristics of Tiele's evolutionary views are mirrored elsewhere. Ernst Troeltsch, the systematician of the *religionsgeschichtliche Schule*, formulated a conception of religious evolution that sought to do justice to the historical, or historicistic, concerns that were quite strong at the time. He said, "To the extent to which we must be quite certain that in religious history there occurs a continuous progress based on the inner human consciousness of the divine spirit, to that extent we can formulate a general concept of religion as the moving force of this evolution and prove Christianity to be its necessary completion."[4] He outlined what he considered the general characteristics of religious evolution: "We can observe a tendency to increasing spiritualization, intensification, moralization, and individualization which is directed to the formation of an increasingly deeper saving faith. . . . Evolution as just characterized finds a place in all the great religions."[5] This tendency toward the general, the human, and the individual and personal which is inferred from the confusion of general religious history reaches its final goal in Christianity (p. 357). As was true for Tiele, Troeltsch conceived an upward movement from the state of being bound to nature to a state of spiritual self-consciousness realized in Christianity. Thus, in Troeltsch, too, we can detect a hidden combination of an idealistic philosophy of consciousness with the modern historical theory of evolution.

This same mode of thought is also found in the work of another member of the *religionsgeschichtliche Schule*, Wilhelm Bousset, who was especially influenced by neo-Friesianism. Bousset provided us with a concise statement of his views: "At first religion arises in a completely gloomy feeling of horror and in the propensity to unconditional surrender, and this feeling develops without plan and often without sense toward each desired object. But then it becomes gradually formed. Religion progresses in the direction of symbols chosen by devotion. The first symbols are the earthly powers that are most important to human life, then the higher forces of nature and the powers of the atmosphere; in the next phase the gods are thought of as governing history. Finally, divinity is sought in the values of the human community and in great persons."[6] Other members of the *religionsgeschichtliche Schule*—Herman Gunkel, for example—sound the same note.

Finally, Rudolf Otto's best-seller, *The Idea of the Holy (Das Heilige)*, made this mode of thought the common property of the history of religions. In Otto's work, religious history is portrayed as a sort of fluctuation between religious predisposition and external impulses. The internal evolution of religion consists of the unfolding of the religious predisposition, deposited in external objectivizations, up to the highest stage of Christianity. Essentially, there is only internal history, since it is internal history that chiefly determines what religion is.[7]

In the last few decades these conceptions have been shattered. Ethnologists and historians, particularly those of the culture-history school, mounted an attack on the optimistic faith in progress.[8] Under the influence of Wilhelm Schmidt, unmistakable theological motives actually led to the propounding of a devolutionary theory (*Urmonotheismus*). In addition, the natural sciences, especially biology, began to revise critically the notion of evolution. Stale and overly subtle theories were relinquished and replaced by new points of view.[9] Yet a third factor was the strong advance of phenomenology and finally of structuralism with its renunciation of a diachronic manner of working.[10] Last but not least, actual political and historical events demolished evolutionistic optimism, perhaps with more force than any other factor.

The dethroning of evolutionary thought in the history of religions is quite apparent in the well-known handbook, *Die Religion in Geschichte und Gegenwart. Religiöse Entwicklung des Menschen* (human religious evolution) appears as an entry only in the first edition. In the second edition one finds instead, under the heading *Religion III*, a critical discussion by Gerardus van der Leeuw of *religionsgeschichtliche Entwicklung* (evolution in religious history). The third and most recent edition contains an article by Gustav Mensching under the same heading. Mensching would like to eliminate the word "evolution" (Entwicklung) entirely and replace it with "change" (Wandlung). Similarly, most recent handbooks of the history of religions have treated religious development or evolution either with skepticism or not at all.[11] The most recent attacks on "development" or "evolution" in the history of religions were set in motion by Walter Baetke and Geo Widengren.[12] Often an old, inherited schema has been preserved, such as that dividing religions into primitive and high religions or into natural, cultural, and world religions.

Timorous and sporadic efforts have attempted to apply the notion of development to the history of religions once again. One of the most noteworthy attempts is that of Heinrich Frick.[13] Frick sought to differentiate between "morphological stage," "historical period," and "level of development." Historical periods are the themes of the histories of specific religions. But morphological stages, in imitation of the morphology of plants, are to be conceived as "growth stages" of a sort. They are not valid generally; they do not describe necessary courses and general regularities. They are simply typological stages that are to be used only in depicting hypothetically the entire development of human religious life.

Mensching follows much of Frick's thought, but, as did Rudolf Otto, he relates development to the knowledge of the holy and its expression, and thus to the changes in that knowledge over time. He rejects the notion of a higher development, that is, of a gradation of value, of progress. A particular religion can only degenerate, it can never get better. Only the idea of religion can evolve to a higher state on the basis of the knowledge of God attained in an individual religion. Mensching wants to conceive evolution as "the development of possibilities given in the totality." "In the es-

sence of religion, as in every living totality, there reside possibilities that become actual, some in one religion, others in
another."[14] Thus, Mensching understands religious history
as the "unfolding of immanent possibilities." But this unfolding reflects only the human, not the numinous side of
religion. It is possible to conceive of a change in religion in
terms of stages only with respect to the ways in which men
react to the encounter with the holy. Such a stage is "a condition that follows necessarily from the essence of religion. It
stands in an essential relation to other sets of conditions that
precede or follow it and in connection with them it forms a
total occurrence." Stages are not bound to a particular chro-
nological succession. They must be demonstrated for each
religious organism. Examples of such stages are the stage of
being bound to the origin—for Frick, the stage of immediacy,
that is, the stage of the direct and unreflective impress of the
numinous; the stage of organization and confessionalism;
the stage of reformation; and the stage of decline.[15]

Insofar as Mensching works with an abstract notion of
"religion" in the singular as the inner side of accidental
religious evolution, he returns to the history of religions of
the nineteenth century. Actually, it is less a return than a
continuation of older work mediated by the activity of Rudolf
Otto. Mensching is heir to both the idealistic philosophy of
consciousness and the liberal Protestantism of the
religionsgeschichtliche Schule.

Such has been the past use of the concepts of evolution
and development in the history of religions. How should we
conceive of development today? "To begin with," said Hegel
in the introduction to his *History of Philosophy,* "one must
ask what development is." He continued, "It is widely
believed that development is a well-known concept and that
discussion of it is unnecessary."[16] Of course, Hegel dis-
agreed. "In connection with development as such," he said,
"we should make a two-fold distinction; we should distin-

guish two states, as it were: the predisposition, the possible, the 'An-sich-sein' (potentia, dynamis) and the actual, the 'Für-sich-sein' (actus, energeia)." The first Hegel compared to the sprout of a plant: it already contains the tree, but it is not the tree itself, since the tree must first unfold, must first develop. Hegel constantly discusses development in terms of the growth of plants (pp. 107–114). He differentiates stages that form a sort of dialectical ladder of progress from the poorer to the richer, just as with the development of plants. "Development only allows that which is originally internal to appear; it only manifests the concrete which was already contained in it" (p. 114). For Hegel, development is unfolding, in motion, living, dynamic. It gives his entire philosophy its character (cf. pp. 106ff).

Hegel's use of the word entwickeln corresponds exactly to German usage and is etymologically correct, as a glance at Grimm's dictionary teaches us.[17] Entwickeln is to unroll, to unfold (explicare). It was used of something produced, of something grown, of something uncovered, or something generated. Similar etymologies underlie the English words evolve, from the Latin e-volvere (to unroll), and develop, from the Old French de-voloper (to unwrap).[18]

Is the concept of development useful in its etymological sense today? Over and again that sense has been used to good effect in the past few centuries. Mensching, for example, identified development (Entwicklung) and unfolding (Entfaltung), without realizing that the two words fundamentally mean the same thing. Still, the necessity of making my last comment shows that the concept of development has itself changed.

Modern biology freed itself long ago from the old notion of pre-formation; it has come closer to a theory of epigenesis. Similarly, the notion of development as a pure unfolding is no longer tenable in the field of history. As the historian Erich Brandenburg has emphasized, history "is not the unwinding of a course of proceedings predestined through the character of the first human embryo, but the work of men who act, who look into the future, and who strive for practical goals and the realization of ideals. They even bring into existence that which is new and could not be calculated beforehand."[19] In a review of Brandenburg's essay, no less a thinker than Friedrich Meinecke has concurred with the indictment of development conceived as unfolding. He proposed that we think instead of development as signifying "an internally continuous series of varying stages and facts that can be ordered according to time conceived ontologically."[20] The effect of the organic concept of development on history has been great and produces fruit even today. Brandenburg emphasized that

> the application of the concept of "development" to human history is in part a reaction to the great wave of biological thought that flooded the human sciences during the Romantic period. It is closely connected with the concepts of "Volksgeist" and "Zeitgeist," above all with the notion that peoples or states may be organisms. In opposition to the Enlightenment, which was increasingly decaying into pure materialism and "mechanism," the allusion to the world of the living was very worthwhile, but its consequences were so unhealthy that it has become common to treat images that made good sense as analogues as if they were the essence of the thing itself and to force far-reaching deductions from them.[21]

Thus, the original sense of "development" is subject to devastating criticism. The question arises whether we should use the concept of "development" in some sense other than the original or whether we should dispense with it altogether. I doubt that the latter course is possible; our only recourse is to use the term in a sense that has already begun

to be used: development as an expression for advance, for
becoming, for motion, for dynamics. In opposition to Brandenburg's attack, Friedrich Meinecke has sought to rescue
"development" for use in the human sciences. He has freed
his concept from organistic and natural-scientific en-
cumbrances and called it "the historical concept of development."[22] In Meinecke's view, one can speak of development
wherever there is an "uninterrupted continuity of activity"
and "any sort of direction toward a particular end that is
defined from within, even if this direction is also dependent
upon and in part determined by external influences as
well."[23] History is an occurrence—*Geschichte ist ein Gesche-
hen*—it is an event, a course of occurrences, an account
about, or rather, an account *of* occurrences. History is becoming in the form of before and after. To that extent, the application of the concept of development to history is no mere "fig-
urative manner of speaking" or "expedient expression," as
Brandenburg supposed,[24] but a consequence of the concept of
history itself. To do justice to the "dramatic" character of history and the creative power of human individuality over
against a notion of evolutionary biohistory that knows no
"creativity active in the midst of becoming," Fritz Kern has
introduced Emile Bergson's well-known expression of "creative evolution."[25]

Meinecke applies to history the notion of continuity in
life rather than causal continuity because the former implies
"a forming principle that proceeds according to a (specific)
shape."[26] He values the individuality of historical forms
highly, and he speaks of development here, too. "Individuality is nothing complete; it is not established for all time.
Rather, it is an active working out of the inner, formative
powers, one of which, but not the only one, is the conscious
will." Meinecke includes communities among forms that develop. Superpersonal tendencies, too, which arise from the
past and determine human activity, can be affected in this

fashion and perhaps altered, hence "further developed."
"Neither human being nor idea can lead an isolated, individual existence." We are, then, concerned not with some natural, necessary evolution but with a "mysterious interaction of
freedom and necessity" that is completely peculiar to all historical life. Meinecke advanced both a microscopic and a
macroscopic way of thinking, the one directed to the activity
of individuals, the other to the creations of the objective
mind that proceed from individual activities.[27]

I have reviewed Meinecke's views in some detail because
they indicate the direction the history of religions will have
to take if it is to make the concept of development useful
once again. They show at the same time that the history of
religions must avoid an antiquated evolutionism which, as
the word itself indicates, rests upon an incorrectly understood, incorrectly applied, and unhistorical concept of development.

To help reclaim the concept of development for use in the
history of religions, I will discuss several levels at which it
may be applied. As a preliminary reminder, let me say once
more that for historians of religions, religions appear historically. As a result, historians must deal only with religions,
not with religion in the singular. The latter is an abstraction
that cannot be found in history. It is, like all abstractions, an
ahistorical phenomenon, which the historian of religion
leaves to philosophers and theologians.

First, let us consider the development of a particular
religion. A particular religion is encountered historically as
heavily entangled with the history of a particular culture, a
particular people, or a particular tribe. As a result, historians
of religions can investigate and factually depict a religion
only in connection with the culture, people, or tribe in which
it is found. Only if historians of religions take account of cultural, social, economic, political, and linguistic history can
they be said to work seriously. To be sure, their work

becomes more comprehensive and complicated if they do so, but historians of religions who pay no attention to these sister disciplines deprive themselves of an important means of understanding and explaining. They destroy the possibility of ever doing justice to the object of their study. I like to relate this continuity between a particular religion and a particular culture to what Meinecke has designated continuities of activity.

In its particular cultural context a particular religion may be said to develop. It participates in the general cultural movement, life, and dynamics.[28] This movement runs its course among different social classes, the lower classes, for example, or the elite. The class structure is an important motivating force in religious development, as can be seen especially among the old folk religions. Treating religion in this way does not mean that one reduces it; it means rather that religion is inserted into the common cultural stream as one current intermingling with others. Each current may play a prominent role in influencing historical development.

Because the development of a particular religion is dependent upon the development of the entire culture to which it belongs, it is hardly possible to formulate periods in the history of a particular religion without referring to the periods of the general history in which it is found. (I concede that to a limited extent there are autonomous religio-historical developments among smaller religious bodies, such as sects, that have no strong ties to the development of the dominant, general culture in which they are found.) This is not to say, of course, that scholars have not tried to formulate religious periods in isolation from their cultural contexts, but whenever they have done so, they have hindered the understanding of religions and have brought disrepute to their discipline.

Similar or parallel stages can be detected among the different individual religions, but these have too often been considered without regard to the general cultural contexts to which they are bound and with too one-sided an orientation toward the so-called world religions.[29] Among such stages we might count the following: the beginning phase, the phase that gives to each religion its characteristic features or "habitus," as W. Baetke used to call it,[30] that is, the stage of founding and consolidation; the stages of adaptation or assimilation ("syncretism"), of substitution (as in the interpretation of the names of foreign gods) or of isolation; the stages of deformation and "encrustation"; of revolution and reformation; a stage of heresies and schisms; and stages of secularization and dissolution. The stage of dissolution, however, can also be a stage of transformation, as when a cult of the gods is transformed into a cult of the saints, and vice versa.[31] One important phenomenon is the transformation of a religion into a "religion of the book," as has happened on several occasions when a nonliterate culture has become literate.

Two elements are especially active as powers determining and motivating religious development. The first is the "habitus" that provides the characteristic features distinguishing a particular religion from all others. The habitus stimulates the adherents to shape a religion and to develop it further in the course of general, historical development. In addition, the general historical development affects the development of the habitus. Religious ideas do not wander through history as ghosts. They become powers in the heads of men that determine their activity, but that have at the same time a regard for the requirements of the environment, of culture, politics, and so on.

These few comments on the development of a particular religion will have to suffice. It is also possible to speak of the development of individual religious forms and teachings. It is on this level that phenomenology has met with much success, although often in an ahistorical manner, as in the works of Gerardus van der Leeuw and Mircea Eliade.[32] Suffice it to say that religious forms cannot be understood apart from their connections with life. In fact, they can be understood only in terms of their connections with life, not in terms of parallel forms more or less closely corresponding to them in other religious traditions. They certainly cannot be understood in terms of a general reasoning.

Strictly speaking, these religious forms have no autonomous development. They are dependent upon the conditions with which they are interwoven. The development of a myth or a cult, for example, arises from its habitus as well as from factors in its historical environment and that environment's own development.

But it is possible to consider religious forms to be relatively autonomous on a variety of levels, and this relative autonomy allows us to speak to a limited extent of an autonomous historical development, for example, the development of a cult of the gods. Proper bounds are often transgressed, however, as they are in the investigations of Georges Dumézil and the Myth and Ritual School. In both approaches, the structuralist tendency, which can be very fruitful, has expelled history. Diachrony has become only a pseudo-history. Removing a religious form from its roots and constructing for it a second-order history or a pseudo-history in the form of an abstract pattern, schema, idea, or whatever, leaves historical reality behind.

It is possible for a religious form to continue or survive within its own tradition, but it may also survive by being taken up and reshaped by another tradition. An example is the concept of the heavenly journey, whose meaning and significance, as Carsten Colpe has shown, is dependent upon the context in which it is embedded and into which it is transferred.[33] Here we can establish clearly how a religious form is dependent upon, or at least influenced by, general cultural development. The "heavenly journey of the soul" is different in Hellenism than it is in shamanism and shamanistic techniques of ecstasy. Even when ecstatic techniques are present, the content and conceptions with which they are bound can vary from culture to culture, or rather, from religion to religion.

The development of a religious form in a single religion can be distinguished from its development in several religions. In the example of the heavenly journey of the soul, for example, development can be traced in a single culture and religion—such as the culture and religion of the Greeks or of Gnosis—but it can also be traced in several religions, where development is shaped by varying contextual factors. Carsten Colpe has done the latter for the heavenly journey rather briefly; Mircea Eliade has done it in much greater detail.[34]

Beyond development of particular religions and of religious forms we can talk about yet a third kind of development: development of groupings that are larger than a single religion or religious form. Inasmuch as religion in the singular is an abstract concept, only philosophy or theology can depict its development. But in a culture that has produced or adopted several religions, it is possible to depict developments in mutual relations that have led to a common unity, as in Hellenism. Such a development can be traced on an even larger scale, as, perhaps, in the Near Eastern-European area over against the Far Eastern-Indian area. Judaism, Christianity, and Islam cannot be understood apart from the religious development of the Near East. On the other side, Buddhism cannot be understood apart from religious development in ancient India and East Asia.

In connection with development on such a large scale, one must be careful not to speak of progress in an evaluative sense. The assumption that Christianity is the *telos* of religious development is a purely theological judgment. A Muslim would certainly disagree. For the history of religions, there is only relative progress, just as there is relative regress.

To be sure, Mensching denied that there could be a progressive development of a religion in the sense of an improvement and claimed that only degeneration was possible, but his prejudice originated in a one-sided orientation toward the world religions. It is possible to speak of an improvement or further development, of an advance (*Fortschreiten*) or "anagenesis" in a single religion. But the criteria for such a value-laden conception are a matter of opinion and not historically verifiable. The development of the concept of God in Egypt and in Israel led by definite stages to a spiritualization and transcendentalization. That is a historical fact, an objectively attested occurrence.[35] But is it progress? For modern Christians, it is, but for a convinced polytheist, it is difficult to say. Historically speaking, it is possible to describe from documents and inscriptions such an occurrence as continuing, even completing preceding conceptions and the religious "habitus." But an evaluation remains in the realm of the subjective, in the realm of the individual's point of view, which is, naturally, determined historically. Judgments of faith are not scientific or historical judgments. They must be excluded from the history of religions.

Finally, we come to development on the largest scale, development in the general religious history of mankind. "The general history of religions," to quote Heinrich Frick, "in analogy to the general history of humanity, seeks to obtain from the individual threads of the historical religions a picture of the general growth of human religious life from remote antiquity on. That cannot be done without a bold, almost poetic synoptic vision encompassing millennia."[36] Here, too, one must guard against an old error, the establishment of stages of development in a manner purely dependent upon religious development. Older historians of religions were led to this error by ethnology and positivism, but these theories of evolution wielded their influence in the history of religions long after ethnology had extricated itself from them.

Today the history of religions can learn from ethnology once again. It can learn how to conceive human evolution in terms of an interplay of economic, social, and cultural history.[37] On these grounds, I formulate my own view of general religious development in terms of stages that portray both functional social systems and phenomenological unities in terms of ideal-typical models appropriate in their own times. First come the religions of hunters and gatherers, then the religions of the planters, next the religions of the pastoralists, and then the religions of those who practice agriculture with the plough. All of these belong to the larger stage of the tribal religions. Next come the religions of the high cultures, first the old folk religions, then the cosmopolitan ecumenical religions. The last stage is that of the world religions, such as Buddhism, Christianity, Manichaeism, and Islam.

I have no doubt that many will raise loud voices in objection to my schema. They will think that they detect merely a new version of an already defeated evolutionism, but that is not the case. I think it possible to overcome the one-sided peculiarities of the older attempts, the distinction between religion and religions as internal and external, the neglect of the entanglement of religions with history as a whole, and the unilinear, evolutionary idea of development. I do not advocate unilinearity—not all religions proceed through these stages—but plurality in a development that is clearly historical and universal in scope.[38]

Between individual stages there are transitions, as one would expect. These transitions can be demonstrated by both the history of cultures and the history of religions. In addition, there are cross-connections within individual stages, but these do not present necessary or generally valid sequences. The real difficulty begins with the rise of the high cultures. From this point on religious forms acquire an even greater multiplicity and breadth than they had before. The increased religious complexity is a heritage of the preceding periods, but it also reflects the increasing complexity of historical events themselves.

A future task of the general history of religions will be to investigate and to depict religio-historical material in regard to a model of universal religious history such as I have just sketched. In recent times, history itself has increasingly set about the same tasks.[39] In contrast to earlier intuitions about human religious history, we must work out a "methodically constructed, rationally demonstrable synthesis" with the help of all interested disciplines.[40] To philosophers of religion and theologians will remain the task of giving an interpretation of the ground underlying such a universal development. Paul Tillich, however, was probably right when in opposition to Max Scheler he separated a stepwise evolution of religion (in the singular) from its actual ascent from below: "No stage," he said, "leads to the unconditioned. Both the highest and the lowest are equally distant from the unconditioned."[41]

Notes

Introduction

1. President's Papers, 1889–1925, The University of Chicago Archives, box 35, folder 2.

2. See his *Die Religionsgeschichte an der Leipziger Universität und die Entwicklung der Religionswissenschaft*, Sitzungsberichte der Sächsischen Akademie der Wissenschaften zu Leipzig, Philol.-hist. Klasse (Berlin, 1962), vol. 107, no. 1; and "Leipzig und die Religionswissenschaft," *NUMEN* 9 (1962): 53–68.

Preface

1. See, respectively, my "Leipzig und die Religionswissenschaft," *NUMEN* 9 (1962): 53–68; "Die Problematik der Religionswissenschaft als akademisches Lehrfach," *Kairos*, n.s. 9 (1967): 22–42; "Das Problem der Autonomie und Integrität der Religions-

wissenschaft," *Nederlands Theologisch Tijdschrift* 27 (1973): 105–131; "Die 'ideologiekritische' Funktion der Religionswissenschaft," *NUMEN* 25 (1978): 17–39; and "Das Problem einer Entwicklung in der Religionsgeschichte," *Kairos,* n.s. 13 (1971): 95–118.

Lecture One

1. Wilhelm Dilthey, *Gesammelte Schriften,* vol. 8 (Leipzig and Berlin), p. 224.
2. In Paul Ramsey and John F. Wilson, eds., *The Study of Religion in American Colleges and Universities* (Princeton, N.J., 1970), pp. 20–21.
3. For a more detailed treatment of this history, see my *Die Religionsgeschichte an der Leipziger Universität und die Entwicklung der Religionswissenschaft,* Sitzungsberichte der Sächsischen Akademie der Wissenschaften zu Leipzig, Philol.-hist. Klasse (Berlin, 1962), vol. 107, no. 1.
4. On Seyffarth, cf. Karl Knortz, *Gustav Seyffarth* (New York, 1886); Georg Ebers, "Gustav Seyffarth: Sein Leben und der Versuch einer gerechten Würdigung seiner Tätigkeit auf dem Gebiet des Ägyptologie," *Zeitschrift der Deutschen Morgenländischen Gesellschaft* 41 (1887): 193–231; and H. Brugsch, *Die Ägyptologie* (Leipzig, 1891), pp. 13, 17f., 157, 168.
5. *Das Evangelium von Jesu in seinen Verhältnissen zu Buddha-Sage und Buddha-Lehre, mit fortlaufender Rücksicht auf andere Religionskreise untersucht* (Leipzig, 1882); *Buddha und Christus* (Breslau, 1884); *Die Buddhalegende und das Leben Jesu nach der Evangelien* (Leipzig, 1882; 2nd ed., 1897); *Die Religion und die Religionen,* pp. 68ff.
6. See, especially, vols. 4–6, *Mythos und Religion,* of Wundt's *Völkerpsychologie,* 3rd ed., 10 vols. (Leipzig, 1900–1920).
7. On Delitzsch, see S. Wagner, *Franz Delitzsch: Leben und Werk,* Beiträge zur evangelischen Theologie 80 (Munich, 1978).
8. Cf. W. Bornemann, "Erinnerungen aus der Studienzeit," *Die Gemeinde* 23–43 (1911): 180–339.
9. See his remarks in *Atti dell' VIII Congresso Internazionale di Storia delle Religioni* (Firenza, 1956), p. 473; and "Zum sakralen Königtum in der Forschung," in *The Sacral Kingship/ La Regalita Sacra: Contributions to the Central Theme of the 8th International*

Congress for the History of Religions (Bonn, April 1955) (Leiden, 1959), pp. 6ff. Outside the world of academia, Jeremias's books —especially his *Das Alte Testament im Lichte des alten Orients* (Leipzig, 1904; 4th ed., 1930) and *Handbuch der altorientalischen Geisteskultur* (Leipzig, 1913; 2nd ed., 1929)—had a large influence on Thomas Mann. See Mann's review of the latter volume (originally in *Vossische Zeitung*, Nov. 17, 1932; now "Die Einheit des Menschengeistes," in Mann's *Gesammelte Werke*, vol. 10, pp. 751–756) and his well-known trilogy, *Joseph und Seine Brüder.*

10. Cf. his *Allgemeine Religionsgeschichte* (Munich, 1918; 2nd ed., 1924), pp. 2, 5.

11. For details, cf. my *Die Religionsgeschichte*, pp. 109–117.

12. *Gudstrons uppkomst* (Stockholm, 1914) [German edition by R. Stübe (Leipzig, 1916; 2nd ed., 1926)]; and "Natürliche Theologie und allgemeine Religionsgeschichte," *Beiträge zur Religionswissenschaft* 1 (1913–1914): 1–109. On Söderblom at Leipzig, see Bengt Sundkler, *Nathan Söderblom* (Lund, 1968), pp. 84ff.; and C. M. Edsman, "Nathan Söderblom in Leipzig," *Forschungen und Fortschritte* 40 (1966): 342–346 (with excerpts from the Söderblom-Archiv in Uppsala).

13. Cf. my "Die Bedeutung von H. Haas für die Religionswissenschaft," *Zeitschrift für Religions- und Geistesgeschichte* 21 (1969): 238–252.

14. The former a rectoral address delivered at Leipzig in 1927; the latter published in *Zeitschrift für Missionskunde und Religionswissenschaft* 41 (1926): 225–239.

15. "Grundzüge einer Phänomenologie des Erlösungengedankens," revised and published under the title, *Die Erlösungsgedanke und seine Deutung* (Leipzig, 1922).

16. According to the minutes of a meeting of the faculty, May 5, 1935, in the archives of Leipzig University.

17. *Mana. Der Begriff des ausserordentlich Wirkungsvollen bei den Südseevölkern* (Leipzig, 1922); and *Die polynesischen Tabusitten. Eine ethnosoziologische und religionswissenschaftliche Untersuchung* (Leipzig, 1930). For Lehmann's later thoughts on these topics, see his "Die gegenwärtige Lage der Mana-Forschung," in *Kultur und Rasse: Festschrift Otto Reche* (Berlin, 1939), pp. 375–385 and "Versuche, die Bedeutung des Wortes *mana* im Bereich des polynesischen Inselwelt festzustellen," in *Festschrift Walter Baetke* (Weimar, 1966), pp. 215–240.

18. See, for example, his review of A. E. Jensen, *Mythos und Kult bei*

Naturvölkern (Wiesbaden, 1953), in *Deutsche Literaturzeitung* 74 (1953): 35ff. (quoted in my *Die Religionsgeschichte,* pp. 56, n. 1; 59, n. 2; 153).

19. *Das Heilige im Germanischen* (Tübingen, 1942). Introduction ("Das Phänomen des Heiligen") reprinted in Carsten Colpe, ed., *Die Diskussion um das "Heilige,"* Wege der Forschung 305 (Darmstadt, 1977), pp. 337–379, and in revised version in Walter Baetke, *Kleine Schriften: Geschichte, Recht, und Religion in altnordischen Schriften,* ed. Kurt Rudolph and E. Walter (Weimar, 1973), pp. 56–84. Cf. also his *Aufgabe und Struktur der Religionswissenschaft* (Gütersloh, 1952), reprinted in G. Lanczkowski, ed., *Selbstverständnis und Wesen der Religionswissenschaft,* Wege der Forschung 263 (Darmstadt, 1974), pp. 133–158, and in revised form in *Kleine Schriften,* pp. 13–27 (Baetke's *Kleine Schriften* contains an introduction to and bibliography of his work).

20. Walter Baetke, *Geist und Erbe Thules* (Göttingen, 1944), p. 5.

21. *Das Heilige,* p. 44 (*Kleine Schriften,* p. 83); cf. *Aufgabe und Struktur,* in *Kleine Schriften,* p. 22.

22. See, e.g., *Das Heilige,* pp. 33–34 (in *Kleine Schriften,* p. 77).

23. From an unpublished memorandum written at the time to the rector of the university.

24. Emile Durkheim, *Les formes élémentaires de la vie religieuse* (Paris, 1912; 6th ed., 1979), p. 4; and Karl Meuli, *Gesammelte Schriften,* vol. 2 (Basel, 1975), p. 1170.

25. Cf. the English translation by Michael Pye in my "Basic Positions of Religionswissenschaft," *Religion* 11 (1981): 98.

Lecture Two

1. See my *Die Religionsgeschichte* (chap. 1, n. 3), pp. 12–16. On Max Müller generally, see J. H. Voigt, *Max Müller: The Man and His Ideas* (Calcutta, 1967); Eric J. Sharpe, *Comparative Religion: A History* (New York, 1975); and R. W. Neufeldt, "Western Perceptions of Asia: The Romantic Vision of Max Müller," in Peter Slater and Donald Wiebe, eds., *Traditions in Contact and Change: Selected Proceedings of the 14th International Conference of the IAHR* (Waterloo, Ontario, 1983), pp. 593–606.

2. See my *Die Religionsgeschichte,* pp. 21–22, and Jacques J. Waardenburg, "Religion between Reality and Idea," *NUMEN* 19 (1972): 131–136.

3. Friedrich Max Müller, *Natural Religion*, Gifford Lectures for 1888 (London, 1889; reprinted, New York, 1975), p. 12.
4. In expanded form in Adolf von Harnack, *Reden und Aufsätze*, vol. 2 (Giessen, 1904), pp. 159–187, concluded in *Erforschtes und Erlebtes. Reden und Aufsätze. Neue Folge*, vol. 4 (1923), pp. 212–213. For a more detailed discussion of Harnack's address, see my "Die Problematik der Religionswissenschaft als akademisches Lehrfach," *Kairos* 9 (1967): 24–28; Carsten Colpe, "Bemerkungen zu Adolf von Harnacks Einschätzung der Disziplin 'Allgemeine Religionsgeschichte,'" *Neue Zeitschrift für Systematische Theologie* 5 (1963): 51–69; and H. Rollmann, "Theologie und Religionsgeschichte," *Zeitschrift für Theologie und Kirche* 80 (1983): 69–84.
5. See the introduction to his *Religionsgeschichtliches Lesebuch* (Tübingen, 1908).
6. H. H. Schaeder, in *Zeitschrift für Systematische Theologie* 9 (1932): 573–575.
7. Joachim Wach, *The Comparative Study of Religions* (New York, 1958), p. 11; Wach writes "linguistically" but means, I think, "philologically."
8. Carsten Colpe, "Bemerkungen zu Harnacks Einschätzung," p. 62.
9. Edmund Hardy, "Was ist Religionswissenschaft?", *Archiv für Religionswissenschaft* 1 (1898): 9–42; reprinted in G. Lanczkowski, ed., *Selbstverständnis und Wesen* (lect. 1, n. 19), pp. 1–29.
10. See chap. 1, n. 19.
11. Cf. chapter 1, note 25. On this usage, see also Richard Pfeiffer, *History of Classical Scholarship, 1300–1850*, 2nd ed. (Oxford, 1976), pp. 183–190; Arnaldo Momigliano, "New Paths of Classicism in the Nineteenth Century," *History and Theory* 21, no. 4, Beiheft 21 (1982): 55–59; and H. Flashar, K. Gründer, and F. Rodi, eds., *Philologie und Hermeneutik im 19. Jahrhundert*, 2 vols. (Gottingen, 1983 and 1984).
12. N. Hartmann, *Das Problem des geistigen Seins*, 3rd ed. (Berlin, 1962), p. 243.
13. Joachim Wach, *Religionswissenschaft: Prolegomena zu ihrer wissenschaftstheoretischen Grundlegung* (Leipzig, 1924), p. 173 (an English translation, which will appear shortly, was not available to me at the time when these notes were written).
14. Ibid., p. 107.
15. Cf. K. G. Faber, *Theorie der Geschichtswissenschaft*, 5th ed. (Munich, 1982), p. 43.

16. Max Horkheimer, *Studien über Autorität und Familie* (Paris, 1936), p. 13 (from K. Ahlström, "Religion und Gesellschaft bei Max Weber," Th.D. diss., Munich, 1972, p. 150).

17. See, especially, H. Sundén, *Die Religion und die Rollen* (Berlin, 1966).

18. Cf. *Les Formes élémentaires de la vie religieuse* (Paris, 1912; 6th ed., 1979), pp. 58–66, 293–342.

19. Karl Marx, *Die deutsche Ideologie* [1845] (Berlin, 1953), p. 126.

20. Richard van Dülmen, "Religionsgeschichte in der historischen Sozialforschung," *Geschichte und Gessellschaft* 6 (1980): 36–59 (quoted from p. 40). A shorter English version of this article has now been published: "The History of Religion as Social Science," *Telos* 58 (Winter 1983/1984): 20–29.

21. See especially Manfred Büttner, "Neue Strömungen in der Religionsgeographie," *Zeitschrift für Missionswissenschaft und Religionswissenschaft* 59 (1973): 33–59, and "Religion and Geography," *NUMEN* 21 (1974): 163–196. Also see, among others, Åke Hultkrantz, "An Ecological Approach to Religion," *Ethnos* 31 (1966): 131–182.

22. Cf. Joachim Wach, *Religionswissenschaft*, pp. 178–179; Ugo Bianchi, *Probleme der Religionsgeschichte* (Göttingen, 1964), p. 15.

23. For discussions of Otto's notions, see R. F. Davidson, *Rudolf Otto's Interpretation of Religion* (Princeton, 1947); V. Lanternari, *La grande festa* (Milan, 1959), pp. 23–38; Michel Meslin, *Pour une science des religions* (Paris, 1973), pp. 68–76; Ugo Bianchi, *The History of Religions* (Leiden, 1975), pp. 169–177; and A. N. Terrin, *Scienza delle religioni e teologia nel pensiero di R. Otto* (Brescia, 1978). The best critical examination of Otto's views from a philosophical standpoint is K. F. Feigel, *Das Heilige* (1929; 2nd ed., Tübingen, 1948). For the mystical background of Otto's ideas, see A. Paus, *Religiöser Erkenntnisgrund. Herkunft und Wesen der Aprioritheorie bei R. Otto* (Leiden, 1966).

24. On van der Leeuw's phenomenology of religion, cf. Eva Hirschmann, *Phänomenologie der Religion*, Th.D. diss., Groningen, 1940; Jan Hermelink, *Verstehen und Bezeugen* (Munich, 1966); Jacques J. Waardenburg, "Religion between Reality and Idea" (n. 2), and *Reflections on the Study of Religion: Including an Essay on the Work of Gerardus van der Leeuw*, Religion and Reason 15 (Amsterdam, 1978), pp. 187–247.

25. G. van der Leeuw, *Religionsphänomenologie*, 2nd ed. (Tübingen, 1955), pp. 773, 774, 775–776.

26. Friedrich Heiler, *Erscheinungsformen und Wesen der Religion* (Stuttgart, 1961), pp. 562–564.
27. Gustav Mensching, *Vergleichende Religionswissenschaft*, 2nd ed. (Heidelberg, 1949), pp. 24–25; therefore, Mensching called Otto's *Das Heilige* "the first, impressive portrayal of a completely new intuition of that divine which enlightens directly" (p. 21).
28. See Rainer Flasche, *Die Religionswissenschaft Joachim Wachs* (Berlin, 1978), esp. pp. 229–249, and my remarks in *Theologische Literaturzeitung* 104 (1979), cols. 18–21, as well as my brief biography of Wach in *Bedeutende Gelehrte in Leipzig* (Leipzig, 1965), vol. 1, pp. 235–237.
29. Cf. W. Baetke, *Struktur und Aufgabe*, in G. Lanczkowski, ed., *Selbstverständnis und Wesen*, pp. 133–137; Th. P. van Baaren, *Voorstellingen van Openbaring Phaenomenologisch Beschouwd* (Utrecht, 1951).
30. Walter Holsten, "Zum Verhältnis von Religionswissenschaft und Theologie," in *Festschrift Walter Baetke*, ed. R. Heller, K. Rudoph, and E. Walter (Weimar, 1966), pp. 191–209 (quoted from p. 192).
31. I am of the opinion that it is both possible and necessary to attain the sort of objectivity demanded by Max Weber, among others—an objectivity grounded in empirical research. See his *Gesammelte Aufsätze zur Wissenschaftslehre*, 2nd ed. (Tübingen, 1951), pp. 148–214, and "Wissenschaft als Beruf," ibid., pp. 572–597. Cf. Dieter Henrich, *Die Einheit der Wissenschaftslehre Max Webers* (Tübingen, 1952).
32. Martin Buber, "On the Science of Religion," in *A Believing Humanism: My Testament, 1902–1965* (New York, 1967), pp. 127–129.

Lecture Three

1. Joachim Wach, *Religionswissenschaft* (lect. 2, n. 12), pp. 9–10, 37ff., 59–60, and especially 113–137.
2. Hideo Kishimoto, "An Operational Definition of Religion," in *X. Internationaler Kongress für Religionsgeschichte, 11.–17. Sept. 1960 in Marburg/Lahn*, edited by the organizing committee (Marburg, 1961), p. 193; C. Jouco Bleeker, *The Sacred Bridge*, Studies in the History of Religions 8 (Leiden, 1963), pp. 36–51. Cf. Robert D. Baird, *Category Formation in the History of Religions* (The Hague, 1971), pp. 17–27. Baird's definition, "Religion is ultimate

concern," which clearly depends upon Paul Tillich, is too broad (cf.
my review in *Theologische Literaturzeitung* 104 [1979], col. 21).

3. R. van Dülmen (lect. 2, n. 20), p. 38. English translation, p. 21.

4. See his "Systematische Religionswissenschaft," *Nederlands Theol-ogisch Tijdschrift* 24 (1970): 81–88, esp. 87–88, and "Science of Religion as a Systematic Discipline," in *Religion, Culture, and Methodology*, ed. Th. P. van Baaren and H. J. W. Drijvers, Religion and Reason 8 (The Hague, 1973), pp. 35–56.

5. See his "The Definition of Religion: On the Methodology of His-torical-Comparative Research," in *Problems and Methods of the History of Religions: Proceedings of the Study Conference . . . on the tenth anniversary of the death of R. Pettazzoni, Roma, 6th to 8th December, 1969*, ed. U. Bianchi, C. J. Bleeker, and A. Bausani (Leiden, 1972), pp. 15–26 (reprinted in U. Bianchi, *The History of Religions* [Leiden, 1975], pp. 201–220).

6. Ibid., p. 26; cf. F. Bolgiani's remarks in the discussion, ibid., p. 29, and his "Per un dibattito sulla 'storia religiosa,'" *Revista di storia e letteratura religiosa* (1969): 1–22.

7. On the Roman conception of "religio," see Walter F. Otto, "Religio und Superstitio," *Archiv für Religionswissenschaft* 12 (1909): 533–554, and "Nachtrag," ibid. 14 (1911): 406–422 (reprinted in W. F. Otto, *Aufsätze zur römischen Religionsgeschichte* [Meisenheim, 1975], pp. 92–130).

8. Cf. Jürgen Habermas, *Erkenntnis und Interesse* (Frankfurt am Main, 1970), p. 238.

9. Cf. the remarkably similar description of religion—stressing com-munity, cultus, myth, belief or faith, and the relation to the tran-scendent—given by Karl Jaspers in his *Der philosophische Glaube* (Munich, 1963), pp. 72, 101.

10. E. Rothacker, *Geschichtsphilosophie* (Munich and Vienna, 1971), p. 27.

11. Cf. Joachim Wach, *Religionswissenschaft*, pp. 137ff., and, more recently, Morton Smith, "Historical Method in the Study of Religion," in Y. S. Helfer, ed., *On Method in the History of Religions*, History and Theory, Beiheft 8 (1969), pp. 8–16. A fuller presentation of my views is given in "The Position of Source Research in Religious Studies," in *The Science of Religion: Stud-ies in Methodology*, ed. Lauri Honko (The Hague, 1979), pp. 98–109 (with comments and discussion, pp. 110–139).

12. See, for example, Jonathan Z. Smith, "Adde Parvum Parvo, Magnus Acervus Erit," *History of Religions* 11 (1971): 67–90 (reprinted in Jonathan Z. Smith, *Map Is Not Territory* [Leiden,

1978], pp. 240–264), as well as other essays collected in *Imagining Religion: From Babylon to Jonestown* (Chicago, 1982).

13. Theodor Schieder, *Geschichte als Wissenschaft* (Munich, 1965), pp. 199ff.; cf. also Reinhard Wittram, *Das Interesse an der Geschichte* (Göttingen, 1958), p. 50. Ernst Troeltsch had already noted, "Comparison can help us grasp particularities better; it has, therefore, good claim to a place among the so-called systematic human studies (*systematische Geisteswissenschaften*)"; cf. *Der Historismus und seine Probleme*, vol. 1 (Tübingen, 1922), p. 191.

14. Th. Schieder, p. 210.

15. R. Wittram, p. 50.

16. Georg Wissowa, *Religion und Kultus der Römer*, 2nd ed. (Munich, 1912; reprinted, 1971), pp. viii–ix.

17. Cf. Schieder, pp. 210–211: Comparison "does not establish a new genre (*Gattung*) but only a method that works alongside other methods of investigation." Cf. also Faber, pp. 43–44. For a different view, see Hubert Seiwert, "Systematische Religionswissenschaft: Theoriebildung und Empiriebezug," *Zeitschrift für Missionswissenschaft und Religionswissenschaft* 61 (1977): 1–18; and J. Habermas, pp. 232–233.

18. Emilio Betti, *Allgemeine Auslegungslehre als Methodik der Geisteswissenschaften* (Tübingen, 1967), p. 95.

19. J. Habermas, p. 321.

20. Cf. K. G. Faber (lect. 2, n. 14), pp. 101–102, 107. On the problem of structuralism in the history of religions, see J. H. Kamstra, "Structuralisme en Godsdienstwetenschap," *Tijdschrift voor Filosofie* 31 (1969): 706–731, and my remarks on Georges Dumézil and Claude Lévi-Strauss in "The Position of Source Research," p. 102–103.

21. E.g., Hans H. Penner, "Is Phenomenology a Method for the Study of Religion?," *Bucknell Review* 30 (1970): 29–34 (limited, unfortunately, to opposing Husserl on theoretical grounds); Jonathan Z. Smith, "Adde parvum parvo . . . ," p. 80, n. 39; Pieter Lamprecht, *De fenomenologische Methode in de Godsdienstwetenschap*, Mededelingen van de Kon. Vlaamse Acad. v. Wet., Lett. en schone Kunsten v. Belgie, K. der Lett. 26, no. 6 (1964), pp. 1–49 (sharp-sighted and critical; with a discussion of particular examples).

22. Cf. C. A. van Peursen, *Phänomenologie und analytische Philosophie* (Stuttgart, 1969). See also Rudolf Boehm, *Vom Gesichtspunkt der Phänomenologie* (The Hague, 1968), esp. pp. 5–14, 119–140, 186–216; and Jacques J. Waardenburg, "Religion between Reality and Idea" (lect. 2, n. 2), pp. 168, n. 105; 171, n. 111;

201, n. 183, who sees no close kinship between van der Leeuw's and Husserl's phenomenology and emphasizes instead van der Leeuw's dependence upon the structural psychology of his day (contra: see my remarks in "Das Problem der Autonomie und Integrität der Religionswissenschaft," *Nederlands Theologisch Tijdschrift* 27 [1973]: 126, n. 51).

23. Cf. Raffaele Pettazzoni, "Aperçu introductif," *NUMEN* 1 (1954): 1–7; "History and Phenomenology in the Science of Religion," in *Essays on the History of Religion* (Leiden, 1954), pp. 215–19; and "Il metodo comparativo," *NUMEN* 6 (1959): 1–14.

24. Geo Widengren, "La méthode comparative entre philologie et phénoménologie," *NUMEN* 18 (1971): 161–172. On Widengren's views, see also his "Problems and Methods of the History of Religions," in *Problems and Methods of the History of Religions* (n. 5), pp. 3–16; and "Some Remarks on the Methods of the Phenomenology of Religion," *Acta Universitatis Upsaliensis* 17 (1968): 250–260. I have set forth my views of Widengren's work at greater length in a review of his *Religionsphänomenologie* entitled "Religionsgeschichte und 'Religionsphänomenologie,'" *Theologische Literaturzeitung* 96 (1971), cols. 241–250.

25. See Åke Hultkrantz, "The Phenomenology of Religion: Aims and Methods," *Temenos* 6 (1970): 68–88; cf. also his "Über religionsethnologische Methoden," in Lanczkowski, ed. (lect. 1, n. 19), pp. 360–393, esp. pp. 377–387.

26. See C. Jouco Bleeker, "The Contribution of the Phenomenology of Religion to the Study of the History of Religions," in *Problems and Methods* (n. 5), pp. 35–45; "Wie steht es um die Religionsphänomenologie?" (review of G. Widengren, *Religionsphänomenologie*), *Bibliotheca Orientalis* 28 (1971): 302–307 (reprinted in C. J. Bleeker, *The Rainbow* [Leiden, 1975], pp. 30–42); and his earlier collection, *The Sacred Bridge* (Leiden, 1963). For a discussion of Bleeker's thought, see Jacques J. Waardenburg, "Religion between Reality and Idea," pp. 183–190.

27. "The Contribution of Phenomenology," p. 41.

28. Cf. Ugo Bianchi, "The Definition of Religion," and A. Bausani, "Islam in the History of Religions," in *Problems and Methods* (n. 5), pp. 55ff.; for a model investigation, see Hubert Seiwert, "Orakelwesen und Zukunftsdeutung im chinesischen Altertum. Eine religionsgeschichtliche Untersuchung zur Entwicklung der Welt- und Menschenbildes während der Zhou-Dynastie," Ph.D. diss., Bonn, 1979.

Lecture Four

1. For the history of the term "ideology," see H. Gouhier, "L'idéo-logie et les idéologies," in *Démythisation et Idéologie. Actes du Colloque . . . Rome, 4–9 Jan. 1973*, ed. Enrico Castelli (Paris, 1973), pp. 83–92 (with bibliography); and Joachim Ritter and Karlfried Gründer, *Historisches Wörterbuch der Philosophie*, vol. 4 (Stuttgart, 1976), pp. 158–164 (under "Ideologie"). On Condillac and de Tracy, see H. Barth, *Wahrheit und Ideologie* (1945; 2nd ed., Frankfurt am Main, 1974), pp. 13–30.

2. Karl Marx and Friedrich Engels, *Werke*, vol. 3 (Berlin, 1962), p. 18: a passage in a part of the manuscript that was deleted.

3. Ibid., p. 143.

4. Ibid., pp. 27, 113.

5. Ibid., vol. 39 (Berlin, 1968), p. 97.

6. Cf. Georg Klaus and Manfred Buhr, eds., *Philosophisches Wörter-buch*, 7th ed., vol. 1 (Leipzig, 1970), pp. 505–506.

7. Theodor Geiger, *Ideologie und Wahrheit. Eine soziologische Kritik des Denkens* (Vienna, 1953; 2nd ed., Neuwied on the Rhine, 1968).

8. Kurt Lenk, "Introduction," in *Ideologie*, 4th ed. (Neuwied on the Rhine, 1970).

9. With this definition I avoid K. Acham's purely pejorative defini-tion (see his *Vernunft und Engagement* [Vienna, 1972]). Acham, who follows Geiger, sees in ideology a "clinging to out of date no-tions," a "semblance of a theory" (p. 21) that lags behind insight that is already possible or that has already been achieved. As a result, its character is that of a regression in the history of thought (p. 216). It must, however, be distinguished from "error" (p. 21). The reference here is to the theory of science and the philosoph-ical (gnosiological) interpretation of the world, not to the general world of concepts that I envision as ideology, into which these enter and play their parts, to be sure, but of which they only con-stitute a part (for example, concerning religion).

10. Cf. Rüdiger Bubner, in *Hermeneutik und Ideologiekritik. Theorie-Diskussion* (Frankfurt am Main, 1975), p. 237.

11. This is common practice in the Soviet Union and East Germany; cf. James Thrower, "The Student of Religion as Critic: A Marxist View," *Religious Studies* 18 (1983): 309–326; "The Study of Religion in the USSR," *Religion* 13 (1983): 127–136; and *Marxist-Leninist 'Scientific Atheism' and the Study of Religion and Athe-ism in the USSR*, Religion and Reason 25 (The Hague, 1983).

12. Geiger, pp. 155–161.
13. See Gustav Mensching, *Geschichte der Religionswissenschaft* (Bonn, 1949).
14. Hans Albert, *Traktat über kritische Vernunft*, 3rd ed. (Tübingen, 1975), pp. 88–89; cf. also his "Hermeneutik und Realwissenschaft," in *Sozialtheorie und soziale Praxis* (Meisenheim, 1971), pp. 42–77.
15. Karl-Otto Apel, *Transformation der Philosophie*, vol. 2, 2nd ed. (Frankfurt am Main, 1981), pp. 122–123, 126–127; cf. also his "Szientistik, Hermeneutik, Ideologiekritik," *Wiener Jahrbuch für Philosophie* 1 (1968): 15–45 (reprinted in *Hermeneutik und Ideologiekritik* [n. 10], pp. 7–44).
16. Hans-Georg Gadamer, in *Hermeneutik und Ideologiekritik*, p. 298, 300, 313–14, and *passim*.
17. For "methodical atheism," as distinguished from "dogmatic atheism," see Rudolf Bultmann, "Protestant Theology and Atheism," *Journal of Religion* 52 (1972): 331–335, esp. p. 332; on "methodological agnosticism" and "methodological neutralism," see Ninian Smart, *The Science of Religion and the Sociology of Knowledge* (Princeton, 1977), pp. 22–23, 38–43, 57–59, 63–73, 158–160.
18. Richard Schaeffler, *Religion und kritisches Bewusstsein* (Munich, 1973).
19. Ibid., pp. 352ff.
20. Ibid., pp. 315ff., 329ff., 387ff.
21. Hans-Joachim Kraus, *Theologische Religionskritik* (Neukirchen, 1982).
22. Dieter Rössler, *Die Vernunft der Religion* (Munich, 1976), p. 25.
23. Ernst Topitsch, *Vom Ursprung und Ende der Metaphysik* (Vienna, 1958), p. 11.
24. Ibid., p. 271.
25. Ernst Topitsch, *Sozialphilosophie zwischen Ideologie und Wissenschaft*, 2nd ed. (Neuwied on the Rhine, 1966), p. 341. Cf. also his *Mythos-Philosophie-Politik* (Freiburg/Breisgau, 1969), and *Gottwerdung und Revolution* (Munich, 1973); as well as the remarkable book (with an implicit critique of ideologies) by A. Demandt, *Metaphern für Geschichte: Sprachbilde und Gleichnisse um historisch-politischen Denken* (Munich, 1978).
26. See my *Die Religionsgeschichte* (lect. 1, n. 3), and G. Stephenson, "Geschichte und Religionswissenschaft im ausgehenden 18. Jahrhundert," *NUMEN* 13 (1966): 43–79.
27. Cf. K. Feiereis, *Die Umprägung der natürlichen Theologie in Religionsphilosophie* (Leipzig, 1965).

28. Hans-Georg Gadamer (n. 16), p. 300; R. Bubner (n. 10), p. 220; Wilhelm Dilthey, *Gesammelte Schriften*, vol. 8 (Leipzig and Berlin, 1931), p. 225.

29. An outstanding example of such a study is H. Cancik's "Christus Imperator. Zum Gebrauch militärischer Titulaturen im römischen Herrscherkult und im Christentum," in *Der Name Gottes*, ed. H. von Stietencron (Düsseldorf, 1975), pp. 112–126.

30. Karl Marx and Friedrich Engels, *On Religion*, introd. Reinhold Niebuhr (New York, 1964), p. 42. Cf. W. Post, *Kritik der Religion bei Karl Marx* (Munich, 1969), pp. 157ff.; and J. Kadenbach, *Das Religionsverständnis von Karl Marx* (Munich, Paderborn, and Vienna, 1970), pp. 176ff.

31. Cf., e.g., R. J. Zwi Werblowsky, *Beyond Tradition and Modernity* (London, 1976); and G. Stephenson, "Zum Religionsverständnis der Gegenwart," *Zeitschrift für Religions- und Missionswissenschaft* 60 (1976): 181–216.

32. K.-O. Apel, *Transformation der Philosophie* (n. 15), pp. 119 and 121.

33. Ibid., pp. 119–120.

34. Urial Tal, in *Concilium* 10, no. 10 (Oct. 1974), p. 607.

Lecture Five

1. E. B. Tylor, *Researches into the Early History of Mankind and the Development of Civilization* (London, 1865), p. 371; cf. esp. pp. 150 ff.

2. Giambattista Vico had already applied the idea of individual development to universal history. Later, we find it in the works of Isaak Iselin, M. A. de Condorcet, J. G. Herder, Goethe, and Hegel (see, among others, Friedrich Meinecke, *Die Entstehung des Historismus*, 4th ed. by Carl Hinrichs [Munich, 1965]; and Rüdiger Schott, "Der Entwicklungsgedanke in der modernen Völkerkunde," *Saeculum* 12 [1961]: 61–122). The idea of interpreting cultures in terms of ages has ancient roots, having been used, for example, by Florus and Augustine (cf. Meinecke, p. 393). In recent times, scholars such as Leo Frobenius, Oswald Spengler, and Arnold Toynbee have used it; others, such as Kaj Birket-Smith (*Geschichte der Kultur* [Zürich, 1948]) and especially Erich Brandenburg (*Der Begriff der Entwicklung und seine Anwendung auf die Geschichte* [Leipzig, 1941]), have rejected it.

3. C. P. Tiele, *Grundzüge der Religionswissenschaft* (Tübingen, 1904). In English, cf. Tiele's more detailed *Elements of the Science of Religion*, 2 vols. (Edinburgh and London, 1897–1899), and his article "Religion," in *Encyclopaedia Britannica*, 9th ed. (1884).

4. Ernst Troeltsch, "Christentum und Religionsgeschichte," in *Gesammelte Schriften*, vol. 2: *Zur religiösen Lage, Religionsphilosophie und Ethik* (Tübingen, 1913), pp. 353–354.

5. Ibid.; p. 351.

6. Wilhelm Bousset, *Die Bedeutung der Person Jesu für den Glauben. Vortrag. Sonderausgabe aus dem Protokoll des 5. Weltkongresses für Freies Christentum und religiösen Fortschritt* (Berlin, 1910), p. 15.

7. Rudolf Otto, *The Idea of the Holy*, trans J. W. Harvey, 2nd ed. (London, 1950); cf. esp. chaps. 15, 17, 18, 20–23. See also Troeltsch's remarks, "Zur Religionsphilosophie. Aus Anlass des Buches von R. Otto über 'Das Heilige,'" *Kant-Studien* 23 (1918): 65–76, esp. pp. 73ff.

8. See, especially, the excellent overview by Rüdiger Schott, "Der Entwicklungsgedanke in der modernen Völkerkunde," *Saeculum* 12 (1961): 61–122 (with bibliography). For further literature, see also my "Das Problem einer Entwicklung in der Religionsgeschichte," *Kairos*, n.s. 13 (1971): 99–100, n. 12.

9. See, among others, Gerhard Heberer, *Allgemeine Abstammungslehre* (Göttingen, 1951), "Deszendenztheorie," in *Die Religion in Geschichte und Gegenwart*, 3rd ed., vol. 2 (Tübingen, 1958), pp. 89–96, and, with L. Schwanitz, *Hundert Jahre Evolutionsforschung* (Stuttgart, 1960). Fritz Kern, *Geschichte und Entwicklung* (Bern, 1951), critically evaluates biological evolutionism and distinguishes four notions of evolution: the logical, the phylogenetic, the axiological, and the ontogenetic. To these, R. Schott, p. 63, adds two more: the integrationist and the additive.

10. Cf. E. Hirschmann (lect. 2, n. 22), pp. 95ff.; and Georges Dumézil's preface to Mircea Eliade, *Traité d'histoire des religions* (Paris, 1949), p. 6.

11. Cf., e.g., Helmer Ringgren and Åke V. Ström, *Religions of Mankind: Today and Yesterday*, ed. J. C. G. Grieg (Edinburgh, London, and Philadelphia, 1966–1967), pp. xxvii–xxix, which rejects the common religio-historical notion of evolution but retains a sort of biological evolutionary idea when it states: "A religion is essentially a living organism which will degenerate if constrained to a static orthodoxy and rigidity regarding ethics and modes of expression" (p. xxix).

12. Walter Baetke, *Aufgabe und Struktur* (lect. 1, n. 19), pp. 141–142, and Geo Widengren, "Evolutionism and the Problem of the Origin of Religion," *Ethnos* 10 (1945): 57–96.

13. Heinrich Frick, *Vergleichende Religionswissenschaft* (Berlin and Leipzig, 1928), pp. 59ff. (cf. Eva Hirschmann's comments in her *Phänomenologie der Religion* [Th.D. diss., Groningen, 1940] pp. 74ff.).

14. Gustav Mensching, *Vergleichende Religionswissenschaft* (lect. 2, n. 25), p. 167. Cf. also Mensching's *Die Religion* (Stuttgart, 1959), pp. 258ff.; his earlier "Religion und Geschichte," *Zeitschrift für Missionskunde und Religionswissenschaft* 44 (1929), pp. 6–11; and his *Geschichte der Religionswissenschaft* (lect. 4, n. 13), pp. 71–72.

15. G. Mensching, *Vergleichende Religionswissenschaft*, pp. 168ff., and *Die Religion*, pp. 307ff. As mentioned earlier, Mensching's article, "Religionsgeschichtliche Entwicklung," in *Die Religion in Geschichte und Gegenwart*, deals more with "change" than with "development."

16. G. W. F. Hegel, *Sämtliche Werke, Kritische Ausgabe*, vol. 15a: *System und Geschichte der Philosophie*, newly ed. by J. Hoffmeister (Leipzig, 1944), p. 101.

17. Jacob and Wilhelm Grimm, *Deutsches Wörterbuch*, vol. 4, cols. 658–659.

18. Cf. E. Partridge, *Origins: A Short Etymological Dictionary of Modern English* (New York, 1983), pp. 150, 789–790. For the roots of the term "development" in Greek and Roman times, see H. Dörrie, "Entwicklung," in *Reallexikon für Antike und Christentum*, vol. 5 (1962), cols. 476–502. The modern term depends on the Neoplatonic conception but is used in a very different sense.

19. E. Brandenburg, *Der Begriff der Entwicklung* (n. 2), pp. 27–28; see also Nicolai Hartmann, *Teleologisches Denken* (Berlin, 1966), pp. 30–31, 51–53.

20. Friedrich Meinecke, "Ein Wort über geschichtliche Entwicklung," in *Aphorismen und Skizzen zur Geschichte* (Leipzig, 1942), pp. 91–113, esp. pp. 93–94 (reprinted in *Zur Theorie und Philosophie der Geschichte*, ed. E. Kessel [Stuttgart, 1952], pp. 102–116).

21. E. Brandenburg, *Begriff*, pp. 27–28. Cf. Kern, *Geschichte und Entwicklung*, p. 19 and n. 4; N. Hartmann, *Teleologisches Denken*, pp. 4, 30–31.

22. Fr. Meinecke, *Aphorismen*, pp. 101, 103; cf. also *Die Entstehung der Historismus* (n. 2 above), pp. 5, 35, 159, 595.

23. Fr. Meinecke, *Aphorismen*, pp. 96–97.

24. E. Brandenburg, *Begriff*, pp. 27–28.

25. F. Kern, *Geschichte und Entwicklung*, pp. 35ff., esp. pp. 50ff.; cf. also N. Hartmann, *Teleologisches Denken*, pp. 52–53.

26. Fr. Meinecke, *Aphorismen*, p. 102; see also *Zur Theorie*, pp. 61ff.

27. Fr. Meinecke, *Aphorismen*, pp. 103, 106, 107, 111; cf. also N. Hartmann, *Teleologisches Denken*, pp. 98–99, 119–125.

28. Here it is possible to make use of the category of "Wechselwirkung" (reciprocity) that N. Hartmann appreciated as nonhybrid (see his *Teleologisches Denken*, p. 90). The notion of reciprocity had already been employed by Herder and Goethe (cf. Meinecke, *Historismus*, pp. 259, 428–429, 542–543).

29. Frick and Mensching are both guilty on this count.

30. W. Baetke, *Aufgabe und Struktur* (lect. 1, n. 19), p. 143.

31. Cf., e.g., Johannes Leipoldt, *Von Epidauros bis Lourdes* (Leipzig, 1957), and Peter Brown, *The Cult of the Saints* (Chicago, 1981).

32. I have, of course, discussed phenomenology extensively in my previous lectures. On Eliade, see my remarks in "Eliade und die Religionsgeschichte," in Hans Peter Duerr, ed., *Die Mitte der Welt* (Frankfurt am Main, 1984), pp. 49–78, esp. pp. 61–69.

33. Carsten Colpe, "Die 'Himmelreise der Seele' als philosophie- und religionsgeschichtliches Problem," in *Festschrift für Joseph Klein zum 70. Geburtstag*, ed. E. Fries (Göttingen, 1967), pp. 85–104.

34. See Mircea Eliade, *Shamanism: Archaic Techniques of Ecstasy* (New York, 1964).

35. Cf. Heinrich Jacobi, *Die Entwicklung der Gottesidee bei den Juden* (Leipzig, 1923); Siegfried Morenz, *Die Heraufkunft der transzendenten Gottes in Ägypten* (Berlin, 1964); and Erik Hornung, *The One and the Many: Conceptions of God in Ancient Egypt* (Ithaca, N.Y., 1982).

36. H. Frick, *Vergleichende Religionswissenschaft*, p. 60; cf. also G. Mensching, *Die Religion*, pp. 80–81.

37. For literature, cf. my "Das Problem der Entwicklung," p. 116, n. 82.

38. On such a notion of development, see A. Heuss, *Zur Theorie der Weltgeschichte* (Berlin, 1968), p. 74.

39. E.g., Josef Vogt, *Wege zum historischen Universum* (Stuttgart, 1961); A. Heuss, *Zur Theorie*; and A. Randa, ed., *Mensch und Weltgeschichte* (Salzburg and Munich, 1969); as well as publications that regularly appear in the journals *Saeculum* and *Cahiers d'histoire mondiale*.

40. F. Kern, *Geschichte und Entwicklung*, p. 70; cf. also A. Heuss, *Zur Theorie*, p. 47.

41. Paul Tillich, *Gesammelte Werke*, vol. 1 (Stuttgart, 1959), p. 376.

Index

Index